Thugness is a Virtue

A Teacher's First Year

in Juvenile Hall

Hannah Wehr

Punk ☆ Hostage ☆ Press

Thugness Is A Virtue
Hannah Wehr

@ Hannah Wehr 2014

ISBN 13- 978-1-940213-99-6
ISBN 10- 1-940213-99-1

Punk Hostage Press
P.O. Box 1869
Hollywood CA 90078
www.punkhostagepress.com

Introduction: Miles Corwin

Cover Design: Geoff Melville

Photo Credit: Brandon Pfarr

Editor: A. Razor

Editor's Acknowledgements

A wise old book peddler once told me, "Every book tells two stories, kid. The first is the obvious one contained between the jackets, the second is the one you decipher on how the writer came to be in possession of the words that made the book happen and the people who were moved by those words enough to help form it into a book." I viewed every book differently after that, reading into the duality of it and most definitely enriching my experience as I read more and more books over the years.

In this book there is an obvious and moving prose about the author and her experience, so profound as it is among the vulnerable, the most harmed who have been labeled by a judgment as the most harmful among our children. The story is framed by the author's personal experience with transcending her own decisions that brought her to the brink in her most vulnerable years of development before adulthood. These pages will lay out that story as well as it can be told, but the other story about how the words came to be in this book is here as well. The author worked hard to document her experience and presented to our publishing concern after we had met her on the stage of a Poetry in Prison workshop that was held at Stories Bookstore in the Echo Park neighborhood of Los Angeles, CA and then again at a repeat of the panel on stage in the theater of Beyond Baroque Literary Arts Center in Venice Beach, CA.

She has been working hard to help give a voice and an opportunity to rediscover a true sense-of-self to disenfranchised youth caught in the societal web of institutional warehousing that has been incapacitating several generations of African-American, Chicano, Indigenous, Asian, Pacific Islander and Central Americans who are underrepresented in politics and economic arenas, but are overrepresented in our prison-industrial-military complex.

This book tells the story of one persons work and indoctrination into working inside a system that exists as we speak in numbers that a far too great to reason that they are doing any good for this world and are potentially scarring our world collectively for generations to come. This story needs to be told and the story of how this book came to be should be understood as well. As publishers we relate deeply to this plight, both of us being products of juvenile institutionalization. We take pride in being vessels for this author's work in this area to expose the realities and give the human face that is necessary for real empathy to occur in those who are more insulated or disconnected from this kind of experience. We find that this book is a great tool to create advocacy and we hope that it stirs others to debate and create into actions a more powerful statement on top of this that will hopefully lead to some empowering changes that could move our society into a closer sync with a greater humanitarian good that might heal some of these ancient wounds we inflict on those who are already playing at life from injured perspectives mired in hopelessness.

A hope against hopelessness, if you will, as simple as that. With that we would just want to state our deepest gratitude for Hannah Wehr in writing this book and allowing us to help disseminate this story so that others might be as moved as we were. We would also want to thank Luis J Rodriguez, Richard Modiano, Miles Corwin, Sandra Hunter, Hugo Machaca, Corrie Greathouse, Geoff Melville and all those in Hannah's family and friends who have supported her dream to give back to those who need it the most at a the time when they seem to be getting the least.

A. Razor & Iris Berry
Punk Hostage Press, 2014

Introduction

I met Hannah Wehr in 2008 when she was a student in a class I was teaching at UC Irvine. While the vision of many college students do not extend beyond their own grades and career prospects, Hannah impressed me because she already had a strong social conscience.

During the quarter she was in my class, Hannah was spending her free time volunteering with the Orange County Probation department, tutoring youths who had been convicted of serious crimes. This made an indelible impression upon her and she soon decided to abandon her goal of a career in children's book publishing for a life helping students who had been neglected and discarded by society – the impoverished, the abused, the incarcerated.

Thugness is a Virtue is definitive proof that Hannah made the right decision. This is a fascinating book about a problematic juvenile justice system, a young teacher's journey, and how she teaches – and learns from – a diverse group of young offenders. Unfortunately, students who need the best teachers are often subjected to the worst. They need teachers who are passionate and intelligent and caring. They need teachers who are tough enough not to be deterred by daunting surroundings and intimidating personalities. They need teachers like Hannah Wehr.

- Miles Corwin, author of *Midnight Alley and Literary Journalism*
Professor at University of California, Irvine

This book is a work of nonfiction. I have changed all names and identifying details to protect the children and adults represented here.

Table of Contents

For all the broken ones.

"Our culture has accepted two huge lies. The first is that if you disagree with someone's lifestyle, you must fear or hate them. The second is that to love someone means you agree with everything they believe in or do. Both are nonsense.

You don't have to compromise convictions to be compassionate."

- Rick Warren

Prologue

February 14, 2001

The first face I see as I regain consciousness is my father's.

"Are you done yet?" He speaks with the exhaustion of a parent who has realized they are ultimately helpless to save their child from themselves. "You should see how horrible you look right now." My father's face is a wall of disgust and pity. I am not sure which is worse.

I can guess how I look: bloodless, wretched, lips black with charcoal, feral and twisted. No one looks their best in the emergency room.

"Where's mom?"

"She took one look at you and collapsed. They put her in the bed next door."

I turn to the thin blue curtain separating me from what I have done. My mother's body folded into grief, broken under the weight of disappointment. What a thing it must be to see your daughter undone by herself. I was not her baby anymore. I was a creature who hurt others just by existing.

"What happened?"

"I don't really remember all of it." It's the truth but it's not close enough to honesty.

"I thought you were at work."

"I was. I got fired. And I called a friend."

My boss had called me into his office today, told me that they had received yet another complaint about me from a customer. "You know why I called you in here?" My boss's large, chapped hands were resting on his gut. There was mustard stains on his shirt and sweat on his red, bulbous face. My manager at this strip mall TGI Fridays is every boss at every chain restaurant.

"I have a pretty good idea." My history here, and at every one of the five jobs I had in the past two years, was pockmarked with disciplinary actions and sit-downs behind closed doors.

"You can't throw salad dressing on customers, Hannah. I can't believe I have to explain this to you."

"He slapped my ass. What did you expect me to do? Let it slide?"

"I expect you to come and talk to me."

"That's not how I work, sir. I handle my own shit."

"Well you can handle your shit elsewhere. You don't work here anymore." He holds his hand out for my nametag.

"Fine by me. Your food sucks anyways."

It's twenty minutes before Kyle rolls up in his white truck. From his jacket he pulls a small plastic bag of green pills. I snatch the bag from him silently. I don't care what the fuck they are. They are something that will make me feel anything besides this, the shit that bored white kids from the suburbs use to kill whatever ennui plagues those who have nothing to complain about.

I chase two of them with cold vodka from the bottle back at Kyle's apartment. His roommate Ben watches me warily as he rolls a joint on the glass coffee table. "You sure you know what you're doing?"

"Worry about yourself." I don't even stop drinking when I speak, my teeth cracking on the glass like ice.

"My girl here can handle it, right?" Kyle slides his arm around me.

Sober, Kyle gave me the creeps. He was the most non-descriptive person I had ever met. There was nothing that hung in the mind when you thought of him, *no scrap of personality to stick to your ribs. He was every community college student who spent too much time with high schoolers. Backward baseball caps, empty eyes of no specific color, fleshy face that never read as anything but enigmatic. Looking into his face was like looking down a ravine that you couldn't see the bottom of. Even though the danger wasn't visible or nameable, it was present and insidious.*

Sitting on the ripped leather couch, the room begins to tilt slowly, a carnival ride in frame-by-frame. An emptiness opens in my chest, one that I could never put enough into.

"You feel good?" He begins to massage my neck, sliding his sweaty fingers between the strap of my bra and my shoulder.

My face is removed from me, my head filling with the kind of fog that causes accidents. "Not really. More weird than anything." I reach for the vodka. Something, anything.

"You probably shouldn't mix the two." Ben's joint dangles from his lip. His eyes bounce back and forth between Kyle and me.

"Shut the fuck up, man," Kyle moves his hand to my thigh.

I stand, not knowing where I am going or where I want to be. All I know is I don't want to be on this couch with him. Nothing is ever the right place, never a safe place to land. A tired bird that sees nothing but water when looking down.

"Let's go in my room." Kyle is already up and guiding me down the short hallway of the apartment, past the Bob Marley and glow-in-the-dark mushroom posters to his room at the end of the hallway. Heavy black blankets are stapled over the windows, a red and orange lava lamp the only light in the black box.

It isn't me that is being pushed onto his mattress. I am outside of this, above it, looking at this faceless man who could have been anyone and this unholy mess of a girl.

"You like this?" His breath is metallic and cloying on my neck.

"It's okay." The walls and the floor pull away from me. I plunge deeper into the center of nothing, everything collapsing into the gravity of this. "I feel really weird."

"Yea, that's some good shit. You want some more?" He climbs on top of me, pulling off his white tank top and throwing it across the room. I touch the large cross tattooed over his heart.

"Do you believe in God?" Words are leaking out of me. I can't grab them. My power is leaving with the language. Soon I will have no words left at all.

"Just relax. This is going to be good." He pulls the earrings from my ears, throwing them in the direction of the milk crate nightstand.

A surge of panic, the only real thing in me, pushes me upward. I scramble to the wall at the head of the bed, trying to cling to it like some sort of savior.

"What's your problem?"

"I don't feel right." My heart is jack-hammering, my breath ragged and painful.

"That's just the shit kicking in. Come here. I will take your mind off of it."

"I want to leave." I can see my pants, but I can't remember how to put them on. Something is wrong. Something is really wrong.

"Fine." Kyle stands up, pulling on his shirt. "If you are going to be a fucking bitch, you can get your own ride."

It isn't Kyle that is grabbing his keys and walking out, leaving the door open. It isn't me sitting against the wall, in panties and a black shirt dotted with small red hearts. It isn't me. There are loud voices coming from the living room.

"You try her. I haven't got time for this shit."

The front door slams. I feel my way down the hallway. Ben is on the couch, smoking his joint. He sees me and his face turns white. He stubs it out on the top of an empty soda can and crosses to me.

"You okay?"

I can only shake my head, detached yet heavy. I drop to my knees on the cigarette stained carpet, unable to understand how one begins to get dressed again. How does one ever begin to get dressed again?

The walk to his car seems to go on forever. Twisting pathways that run through the labyrinth of the apartment complex. There is a pool and children are running and screaming and splashing. I am underwater, everything removed and blurry. This isn't me. It can't be. I am here and I am not here.

In the car, the freeway flies by us, beneath us. Raging and roaring like waves, unending and urgent. The cars are flying. Flight. Taking flight. I begin to open the door, when a hand catches the back of my shirt.

"What the hell are you doing? Stay in the fucking car!" Ben's anger eclipsed by fright. He doesn't know what to do with this, with me.

I can only stretch my arms out towards the blur passing us, aching to fly and float like everything else is. Ben doesn't let go of me until we have pulled up in the ambulance bay of the hospital. My legs give way as I get out of the car. I grab the door handle and struggle to remain upright. A woman with a bloody bandage wrapped around her wrist gives me a look, curious and concerned, as she enters the ER. Ben guides me inside, up to the nurse's desk. Before we reach

19

the glass, I turn to him.

"Go." The word falls from my mouth like a stone. It hits the linoleum between us. I look at it there. It's more of a question, really.

"Are you sure?" Ben pauses, still holding my arm.

"I don't want you to get in trouble."

He lets my arm go and walks out of the waiting room. He doesn't look back.

"Miss, can I help you?" The nurse is calling me from the window.

I walk up to the glass and open my mouth to speak. My legs give way, everything goes black, and I drop to the floor.

The man standing above me when I open my eyes is fully sleeved, brightly colored flowers and skulls reaching from his thick wrists up into the sleeves of his scrubs. A large woman with frizzy hair and pink scrubs is cutting off my clothes with scissors.

"I'm dying," I whisper. I can feel it. This is what death must feel like. Insistent, frightening, yet accepting. All are welcome here.

"Not on my watch." He slides an IV into my arm, a trickle of blood running down and pooling in the bed sheets.

"Drink this." The pink-smocked woman puts a paper cup in my hand. My fingers don't do what I want them to and it falls to the floor, gritty black liquid splashing everywhere.

"Shit." The woman throws down her scissors and storms out of the room.

The man throws a towel over the black puddle. His black hair is buzzed down to a shadow of its former self. His square tan face is lined and tanned, like old luggage.

"I'm sorry," I mutter.

"It's okay. You're dying, remember? You are allowed to spill shit."

"Am I really dying?"

"No. You took some pills and you had a bad reaction to them."

The nurse returns with another paper cup. This time, she holds it to my lips and pours it into my mouth. It tastes like liquefied asphalt. I gag and choke, black ooze dribbling out of my mouth and nose.

"Activated charcoal," she murmurs, through pursed lips. "This will help deactivate whatever you took."

I fall back into the pillow, tears rolling down my cheeks. I want my mom. I feel four years old. The first time my parents left me with a babysitter for the night, I sat on their bed, knowing that because they were letting me watch TV when I wasn't sick, they were up to something. My mother got dressed up, casting guilty glances at me. Even as a preschooler, I could read between the lines. When they left, I felt like they would never come back. A cloud of fear and abandonment settled in my little chest. That same feeling was returning now.

"We called your parents. They are on their way." *He sticks the EKG leads to my chest. I look at the cabinet as he does.*

I am terrified of what they will say and do, how horrified and disappointed they will be. But I am even more terrified that they won't come. I have done so much damage these past few years. The countless suspensions and eventual expulsion from the same school my mother worked at, the fights at school, the older guys and late nights and screaming, the lying and the sneaking out. I lashed out at parents, teachers, therapists, concerned friends that were pulling away. If you tried to help me, I wanted nothing to do with you.

"Why do I feel this way?"

"Is this an existential question or are you talking about the shit you took?" His smile is sad and resigned.

"Those pills." What was in those fucking things? This was not my first time experimenting with drugs, but I had never felt anything like this.

"The ecstasy? It's laced with heroin and meth. We have had a few teens come in over the past month with the same reaction. It's starting to become rather old hat."

"Sorry. Next time I will try to take something new and keep shit exciting for you."

"At least your sense of humor is in order." He flips on the heart monitor by the bedside. A thin green line appears and then begins to jump erratically, sharp peaks and sudden, angry valleys glowing on the monitor. "Well, this is probably why you are feeling out of it. You are in an arrhythmia."

"That's a bad heartbeat, right?" I crane my neck to get a better glimpse, but it's all cardiac Greek to me.

"Your heart is throwing out an extra beat after every normal one. That's the meth that was in the pill. It does crazy stuff to your heart."

"Not even my heart can get it right."

"The best of us have the worst of hearts." He turns the monitor so I can't see it.

"What about feeling all underwater?"

He is smiling at me and I realize I am doing pantomime swimming motions. "That's the heroin."

The charcoal kicks in and I throw myself over the edge of the bed, vomiting violently onto the man's shoes.

"Nice aim." He shakes his feet, sending black liquid spattering outwards *onto the cabinets.*

"I am so sorry." It takes all my strength to push myself up on my forearms. Every part of me is wasted and drained; there is nothing more that I can fight against or with.

"It happens. I keep an extra set of shoes in my locker for people just like you."

"I didn't know there were other people like me."

"You think you are the first sixteen year old who tried to deal with bad feelings by taking drugs?" He grabs a Kleenex from the counter and dabs at my face.

"What do you know about that?" I roll my face away from him. If there is anything I don't want, it's kindness. I can handle anything but that.

His silence makes me turn back. "No one gets sleeves unless they have to cover something up." He smiles sadly, proffering his arms, palms up, to me. Under the dark blue flowers and nautical designs, there are so many scars.

"How did you get from that to here?" It seems a daunting road to head down. To change means to acknowledge that something wasn't working. I know my life for the past few years has been a messy, selfish, and dangerous one, but it still scares to me to have to admit to myself that it was actually a disaster. When you fail at your own life, where do you go from there?

"I just decided one day that I was done hurting people and I wanted to start helping them. So I cut out what and who I needed to cut out."

"Were you lonely?" The blood pressure cuff beeps and constricts around my arm.

"At first. Your phone will stop ringing for a while. And then you will meet new people and your phone will start ringing again, but for the right

23

reason." He takes a seat on a black stool beside the gurney, sliding a pulse oximeter onto my finger with the gentleness of a proposal.

"I don't know if I am brave enough for that."

"You just have to make up your mind that you want to be a better person more than you are afraid of becoming one."

"But you don't know what I have done. It's not like I can make that shit just go away."

"No one can. But our past doesn't have to determine our future." He stares directly at me in a way that makes me feel more seen than I ever have. Gazes that hit like a good swift left to the jaw undo me.

"Why did you choose medicine?"

"We all have a calling. This was mine."

"I don't know that I have a calling yet. I mean I am not really passionate about anything." It was weird to say this and even weirder to finally realize that was the root of the constant empty feeling in my chest.

"You ever think about working with troubled youth?"

September 7, 2010

I have been in town for less than an hour and I have already been assaulted by an angry Chinese woman wielding an umbrella in the middle of a Safeway.

"Line! There is line!" She swats my leg with her parasol.

"I really wouldn't do that if I was you." I am choosing my words very deliberately. "Now take your baby sun hat and your umbrella and go figure out exactly what type of weather you should be dressing for."

In the parking lot I throw my frozen TV dinner and cheap bottle of red wine into my car. Raw as steak tartar, I crumple into tears.

Long car trips exhaust me. Sitting in one position for hours on end is as close to torture as I have experienced, especially when the route is straight up the 5 freeway through lovely spots such as Bakersfield and Fresno with nothing but a bag of pretzels and the occasional pensive-looking cow to keep me entertained.

That morning I had thrown my life into my gray Civic and driven all day to my new home in Northern California. My knowledge of Northern California is the same as my knowledge of campaign finance reform or the Mormon Church: I am aware of it. I knew exactly one person who lived in the top half of this state, having spent the past 26 years of my life in the Southern part. The last time I was up here, I was four and I fell off a carousel and onto my head. This is my Northern California scrapbook: head injuries and abusive Asian women.

I am going to jail. Juvenile Hall, to be exact.

When I was finishing up my teaching credential program at UC Irvine, I started throwing out fishhooks for a job. It didn't take me long to realize that if I wanted to actually utilize my teaching degree, I was going to have to move out of Orange County. Teaching jobs were scarce, to put it mildly. Out of the 200 of us that were completing our teaching credentials, less than a dozen in the English program would get jobs.

There was an offer to teach in Hungary and another at a school in the California high desert that was known more for its meth consumption than anything else. *Breaking Bad* hadn't yet been created, so I didn't yet recognize the full potential of methamphetamine. Hungary was appealing, mostly because I practiced saying 'the year I lived in Hungary' over and over and I liked how cultured it made me sound.

I had two years of experience as a mentor and tutor with incarcerated youth in Orange County, so when I saw an opening at a school in a juvenile hall I jumped on it. It felt like finding your home in another place, like finding someone from your tour group when you are lost at Disneyland. Within three days I had said goodbye to everyone, put my life into boxes and suitcases and secured two weeks in the type of seedy hotel that you see on Cops. I was essentially homeless and about to be spending a lot of time with criminals.

*****

I had flown up to this area a few days before my move to sign my final paperwork for the new position and to visit my classroom. The new head of the school, Nikki, had taken on her post about three weeks ago so there was a feeling of change in the air, a sense of a turning tide. I was also advised during my official job offer phone call, four days before school actually started, that the school was implementing a whole new curriculum which I was expected to verse myself on within the next few days. The school was in a rapid revolution: new administration, new teachers, new curriculum. I felt like I was either coming into this job at the best or worst possible time.

I was laying on the motel bed, wondering how many germs were on the remote control when I received a phone call from Nikki.

"Come out to the school site. You need to get the lay of the land."

"I don't have a car. Or know how to get there."

"Just get a cab. They will know how to get here."

Of course. People must ask to go visit juvenile hall every day.

A phone call to the front desk got me a taxi and the taxi brought me a young man of vaguely Middle Eastern descent who had clearly not been a taxi driver that long and was not at all familiar with the area. All I had was an address that didn't register when Mapquested, so I back seat navigated via guesstimated directions from Nikki on the other end of my phone. There was a lot of 'turn here...no wait! Shit! U-turn!'

Finally the taxi rolled up to the top of a hill, into the parking lot of juvenile hall. Tall, sterile, menacing; it was exactly what you would picture an incarceration facility to be in a fairly well-to-do county. Roughly oval shaped, the massive two-story building was modern, sharp-edged and beige, dotted with windows and surrounded by high, barbwire-crowned fences. It was as if the architects of Jurassic Park had branched out into school construction. The parking lot was clean and empty, save for one car in the principal's parking space. The grass between the fence and the building was tall and crispy brown, barely stirring in the dry heat of late August.

The taxi driver gripped the steering wheel with both hands, craning his neck up to look at the top story of windows in the cellblock. "I have never brought anyone here before." His voice shook a little.

"I would assume most people that come here are brought in by the cops."

"Yes, that makes sense. You don't need me to stay do you? Or to come back for you?" His tone was begging me to say no.

Nikki met me at the door, in an outfit that screamed Coldwater Creek and powder that was two shades too light. Her hair had been dyed too many times and was verging on burgundy. Her round, doughy face was creased with lines and the exhaustion that comes with working with teenagers for three decades. She looked over my shoulder as she smiled.

We walked into the front office: desks, computers, cubicles, women talking on phones. Gray partitions between each workspace, only two of which were occupied. It would be a totally average office if it wasn't for the sallyport that served as the bridge into no-mans land. There were little potted plants wilting slowly next to computers, the requisite 1994 'Good Posture for Computer Users' brochures tacked up to the walls, the glaring fluorescent overhead lighting. An older Asian woman with thick black hair and a soft, pale face squinted at me as I passed her cubicle before turning back to the glare of her screen.

"Leave your purse in one of the lockers. No bags go through the sallyport. That includes your phone and keys." There was a battered row of beige lockers against the wall beside the sallyport entrance. Gray locks hung from half of them, the rest open like terrified mouths.

I followed Nikki into the sallyport, a small room between two locked doors that could only be buzzed open by the control booth that served as the brain of the hall. In the small space, monitored by cameras, Nikki and I waited as one door was buzzed shut before the second could be buzzed open. This little space, no bigger than the bathroom in my motel room, is a claustrophobic's nightmare. There is no way to leave; you are trapped in a concrete box, your exit subject to the whim of whoever is in the control booth. As a lifelong despiser of small spaces, I could feel cold sweat start to break out on the back of my neck. My face began to burn and the edges of my vision went black and blurry. Shit, if this was going to happen every time I had to cross through, this was going to be an issue.

"So how many times a day do we have to do this?" If I have one defining characteristic, it's that I always take the stairs over the elevator. I once saw a movie where the guy pushed the emergency button to stop the elevator so he could propose to his girlfriend. It was supposed to be romantic but all I could think of was that if a guy did that to me, he would be walking out of there single.

"At least six times a day, assuming you don't forget something on one side or the other. No one passes through any doorway here without being watched by control." Nikki leaned against the wall and pointed towards the camera mounted in the corner of the sallyport.

As we waited in the sallyport, I asked Nikki about the last teacher, the one who I would be replacing. The opening had come up very suddenly, in late August. Most teaching posts are listed in May. I was trying really hard to just look and act normal. Nikki thankfully seemed so detached and distant, that she wasn't registering my heaving chest or flushed face.

"I guess I should tell you before the kids do." No good news ever follows a statement like this.

There was a loud mechanical buzz and Nikki leaned into the door, pushing it open. Relief gushed through my limbs. Survived the first challenge: a room. Way to go, Hannah. We walked into a long hallway, flanked on one side by windows facing a football field and more buildings surrounded by high brick walls and barbed wire. The other side of the hallway was lined with classrooms. The walls were whitewashed brick, a few faded motivational posters and informational fliers on how to seal criminal records were posted up.

Nikki still hadn't answered my question about the last teacher, but judging by the look on her face, she was trying to formulate the right way to phrase it. She unlocked the classroom to the right of the library. It was a big room with whitewashed concrete walls. Desks were an arms length apart, as they often are in facilities that teach violent offenders. There was, of course, no stapler on the desk, no pushpins in the walls. Nothing that could be made into a weapon. The only windows were small and placed directly beneath the line where the ceiling connected with the wall. Too high up for any kid to try and break through. The space was large, cold, and foreboding. The ceiling vaulted up and away from the windows, crisscrossed with air conditioning ducts and vents. Two walls had large white boards and a third, a rolled up projector screen. All of the desks were inexplicably facing away from it. There was a bulletin board that someone had taped a few mismatched sheets of colored construction paper to. A piss-poor attempt at bringing a little color into this sanitarium. Aside from the twenty beige desks, it felt more like a plus-sized jail cell than a classroom.

"The lady who you are taking over for died." Nikki sat on the edge of the teacher's desk by the door, flipping through her emails on her phone. "She died here. In this school."

"She died in front of the kids? I am going to be stepping into a dead woman's shoes?"

Pocketing her phone and flipping her bangs out of her eyes, she adds, "She died here at school in front of the students from a stress-induced brain aneurysm. She was thirty-four. How old are you again?"

There was a bright red button in the middle of the wall that stood out against the white gloss, bright as a poppy. My first instinct was to press it and see what happened. Nikki held out her and hand and shook her head.

"Those would be your 'Code Orange' buttons. If a kid attacks another kid, just press one and it sets off the alarm system and the guards will come running."

"Does this happen often?"

"Well from what I have been told, it used to happen all the time. Now they split the classes by gang affiliation, so there are less assaults."

"Not by grade?" Thirteen year olds and eighteen year olds in the same classroom? How the hell was I supposed to teach them anything? "What about lesser, non-violent disruptions? Do we do detention and suspensions and so forth like a regular school?"

"Not exactly. Minor infractions receive a Time Out, which is when the student is removed from school for one period. A more severe infraction is a Dismissal From School. A DFS means that the student is not allowed to come to school for a few days. You need to watch these kids really closely. They will steal anything that isn't bolted down."

"That seems a rather gross generalization."

"You're in jail, remember?" She was already getting cross with me. This was the going to be the beginning of a beautiful friendship. "Never turn your back to them. Don't let them use anything that could be a weapon."

"Does that include pencils?"

"You will do fine. Just don't trust them. These are not good kids. None of them are here because they were knitting too loudly in church. I have to go do some work. Why don't you get settled in?" And with that, Nikki was gone.

Pulling open every drawer and cabinet revealed that this place had been gutted like a condemned house. No pencils, glue sticks, construction paper, not even the books that I was supposed to begin teaching my students out of next week. The last teacher's stuff had apparently been cleared out after she died. There was an ancient computer and an even older overhead projector that was shoved under the desk, both coated lightly with dust. This place needed a plant. Hell, even a stick would brighten it up.

The blind leading the blind. I had never been a kid in jail. How was I supposed to relate to them? We weren't even from the same area, let alone socioeconomic demographic. I had only a few troubled teen years to connect me to them and I certainly wasn't about to start digging up stories of drugs and stealing to try and form some kind of a bond with these kids. And bonding with them via education wasn't looking too hot either as I had none of the supplies that I need. Hey kids, lets read a book...oh wait, we have none. What was the bell schedule? How many classes would I be teaching? Were there block periods? Were there even any other teachers? I hadn't seen a soul besides Nikki. I didn't even have a keycard to get into the locked-down building. I literally couldn't get into my own work without help. Maybe not the blind leading the blind exactly; more like the myopic and inexperienced leading the misguided and incarcerated.

"You the new English teacher?" A sun-tanned woman wearing a Hawaiian print t-shirt and track pants appeared in my doorway. "I'm Sara! PE teacher! Has anyone showed you around the housing units? No? Come! I will give you a tour." She was very warm with a slight rasp to her voice. Her strawberry blond hair was pulled back into a ponytail, a leather fanny pack hanging loosely about her generous hips.

I followed close beside her, grateful to leave the cold, sterile hush of the school and step into the warmth of the track and field area, the fake grass clean and short as military hair. We proceeded up the perimeter of the oval track that ran perpendicular to the housing units. Sara took long, fast strides so I had to walk rather briskly to keep up with her gait.

Despite the modern style of the facility, there was nothing cheery or welcoming about the housing units. They were beige, surrounded by brick walls fifteen feet high, topped off with five more feet of chain link fencing and crowned with circular metal spikes and flanked by patches of dirt and brown weeds. Even the plants here were being punished.

"These are the units where the older boys live. They are split by the length of their sentence. Less than ninety days on the left and more than ninety days on the right. Nortenos and Surenos are mixed in all the units." She gestured to a large building on our right. Bricks on top of bricks, the metal fencing and barbed wire twinkling like tinsel.

At this point, she had pretty much lost me. I could guess that Nortenos and Surenos must be rival gangs, but aside from that I had no idea what she was talking about. Gang life was as foreign a country to me as Croatia. I opened my mouth to ask for an explanation but she pushed forward in the tour. "Next, we have the younger boys' unit, which shares a wall with the girls' unit." We walked past the second conjoined building. Each half of the unit had a separate entrance down a brick-wall flanked corridor to a locked door. The glass on the doors was heavily tinted, making it difficult to see anything aside from a few blurry shapes.

A bloom of worry opened in my chest. My experience had always been with male inmates. Three-fourths of the young inmates that I have worked with over the years had no paternal figure in their life. Either by death, drugs, prison, or abandonment, these children were raised by a mother, sometimes a grandmother. As a result, most of them had a deep respect for women who were older than them as they were synonymous with maternal energy. My own kind terrified me. I know firsthand the drama, emotional shakiness, and catty infighting that came with being a teenage girl. Teenage girls should thank their lucky stars that their parents don't send them all off to Siberia the day they turn thirteen.

"And these units...well you won't be dealing with those kids. They don't come to school." Sara stopped in front of two units that were located up a small hill, distinctively removed from the other units. "Direct files, they are called. The ones who have killed or are being charged as adults."

A door in the side of the brick wall leading the housing unit opens and a short, stocky guard in all black walks out, accompanied by a black-haired teenager in a pale yellow shirt. Sara raises her hand in a greeting to the guard, who raises his slightly. The thin Latino boy next to him walked with his hands clasped behind his back, squinting at the sun.

"You want to see the inside of one of the units?" Sara led me into the first housing unit we had passed before I had a chance to answer. She pushed the small metal button positioned beneath an intercom beside the door and we waited.

"I see a lot of waiting for doors to open in my future."

"Yea, you get used to that. It definitely teaches you patience. Come to think of it, a lot of things here will make you patient. Nothing happens quickly or smoothly."

The inside of the housing unit looked like Gymboree had opened up a privatized prison. The housing unit was massive, two-storied and carpeted. The painter seems to have had some sort of multiple personality disorder. One wall was light yellow, another baby blue. The windows at the base of the ceiling rimmed in rusty red, matching the staircase and the railings that line the second story walkway. The lavender guard's station is lavender was surrounded by mint green brick walls. Circular metal tables, each with four attached seats were scattered in pods throughout the unit. T Green cell doors, each with a thin window in it, dotted the two story high walls. The ceiling was covered in metal paneling, spotted with can lights.

Two men were seated at the guard's station, elevated a few steps up from the floor and surrounded by waist high walls. They waved at Sara. One was slender and attractive, a light-skinned African American with attentive brown eyes. The other guy is short and stocky, his blond hair sheared closely to his square head. He had those kind of eyes that you just know were heart-stopping twenty years ago. A slight smirk flickered across the blond guy's face as he took in my inexperience and low-grade terror that read like a traffic light.

"You want to meet the boys?" Sara grinned mischievously.

"I guess I have to at some point."

Past the guard's station was a glass-walled room recessed into the wall filled with chairs. And the chairs are filled with bodies. Holy shit. These are them. These are my kids.

They collectively turn their heads from the television they are watching and take me in. A few throw a wave up to Sara. The boys are everything and nothing I had expected. They are all sizes and shapes, some short and stocky and others lanky and lean. Most of them are Latino with a handful of African-American, Caucasian, and Polynesian thrown in. There are buzzed heads and long black braids. Brown eyes and hazel ones, some obscured behind glasses. Faces marked by pimples and scars and tattoos; these boys are all boys. I could walk by any of them on the street and nothing would scream criminal or make me want to cross to the other side. Each

33

boy is so different not just physically but even in how they look at Sara and I. How they sit and arrange their limbs in these plastic chairs, the way their eyes snap and process this new person. I can't, at first sight, find any common denominator. Except for the blue sweatshirts and pants and the white shoes with Velcro straps that are marked property of the county, these boys could be anyone's brother, friend, cousin, son.

September 9

The night before my first day, I do my homework on the whole Norteno and Sureno thing. Surenos are members of Mara Salvatrucha (MS 13), which is pretty much the most dangerous and powerful Latino gang in the world right now, with members throughout South, Central, and North America, as well as parts of Europe. MS 13 started back in the 1980's with Salvadorian immigrants in Los Angeles banding together against other established gangs in the area. MS 13 began recruiting Hispanics from various backgrounds, many of which were illegal immigrants. As these immigrants got deported back to their homelands, they carried back the message and the vision of MS 13, which lead to the gang opening up chapters throughout most of Mexico, Central America, and South America. To date there are about 50,000 members with one fifth residing in the United States. Their counterpart, the Mexican Mafia, was formed in 1957 and functions largely in prisons. Both of these factions are at the bottom of the Sinoloa Cartel hierarchy, which is the largest and most powerful drug trafficking organization in the world. MS 13 members are easily identifiable through their adopted symbolism: the letters M and S and the number 13 or XIII. The founding members were fans of heavy metal and adopted the devil horn hand gesture often thrown up at concerts as their own due to its similarity to the letter M.

The origins of Nuestra Familia (Our Family) are a bit hazier. The gang got its start in the late sixties in either Folsom or Soledad Prison. The Mexican Mafia was the main Latino gang in California's prison system in the late 1950's and 1960's. They were running things, ostensibly protecting Latino rights in prison. But they were notoriously disrespectful to the migrant workers from Northern California who banded together to form Nuestra Familia. Nuestra Familia was composed of Nortenos, or Northerners, and their sworn enemies were now the Surenos, or Southerners.

There was an incident called 'The War of the Shoes' which brought more manpower to what is currently the largest and longest running Latino gang rivalry in California's history. In prison, your shoes represent your masculinity and self-respect. If someone takes your shoes, it is a sign to other inmates that you are weak, unable to fend for yourself, and you will be open to everything from harassment to beatings to sexual assault. A member of Nuestra Familia had his shoes stolen. A Crip took pity on him and gave him a pair of shoes to protect him from victimization. This lead to the Nortenos and Crips clicking up in the California prison system.

This rivalry between Northerners and Southerners has intensified dramatically over the decades with bloodshed becoming commonplace and kids as young as ten getting involved in the lifestyle, usually as a result of pressure from family members who have already taken a side.

The main thing separating these violent rivals was location. Their ethnicity, their root values, even the state they were from was the same. There was an invisible line drawn somewhere around Delano, California that split the state into two rival factions. Basically where you happen to be born dictated who you die for and who you vow to kill.

My classes would be broken up by gang affiliation and hopefully this would keep the rate of assaults to a minimum. I have never actually seen a gang fight before. When I was volunteering in the facility in Southern California, they only let one boy out to work with me at a time. Often the boy was shackled, hand and foot, to the chair he was placed in. At least this place didn't shackle the kids during movie time.

Aside from the Nortenos and Surenos, there would also be the infamous Crips and Bloods to contend with. And a fifth gang, a smaller African-American faction called, hilariously, the Taliban. A relatively new gang, it was started in the Bay Area Peninsula in 2002 and focused on the standard gang staples: violence, intimidation, guns and narcotic trafficking, and generally just terrorizing the cities its members inhabited.

Browsing through the thousands of news articles having to do with Northern California, there is one city that keeps popping up over and over: East Palo Alto. I have never heard of this city, but there is a lot of homicide going on there and it is home to dozens of different gang factions. And if I want to know my students well, I have to go to the city they live in and die for.

September 10

"I Have Confidence" from *The Sound of Music* is on repeat during my misty first day drive to work, my hope being that this will take my anxiety from a rolling boil to a light simmer. If Julie Andrews can deal with Nazis while singing and rocking a bad haircut, I can deal with anything.

The hilltop compound is shrouded in thick fog, like a scene out of a horror movie. A few turns up a winding road, past signs reminding me that I should not be here if I was not authorized. Having no keycard or probation identification badge yet, I really hope no one questions who I am or why I am here. If a sweaty, terrified stranger showed up at my work, I would probably try to lure them into a closet and barricade the door until the authorities arrived.

I sit for a moment, trying to slow my heartbeat. My hands are clammy and the urge to turn around and drive the seven hours back to Orange County is slamming in my temples. The long-term boys housing unit is separated from the teacher's parking lot by a double barbed wire fence. The massive, two-story building looms down from its elevated position atop a small hill covered in dead grass and sticks; everything has died trying to get here. *I have confidence in sunshine/ I have confidence in rain.*

A kick of wind pushes the gauze of fog from the windows. In each one is the outline of a body, softened into anonymity by mist and distance. I stare back up at the dozen or so blurred faces that are trying to figure out who I am and why I am here. It is less daunting than one would think. The bodies themselves actually lessen the sinister, inhumane presence of this correctional behemoth. Even from where I stand, I can tell it's not menace these kids are conveying, only curiosity.

The door to the office is inaccessible without a keycard. I bang on the glass, trying to make my knock sound polite yet audible and realizing this is impossible. A woman with a chrysanthemum of wild red hair and layers of beaded necklaces comes bustling up to the door, takes one look at me standing at the door looking like a walking panic attack, and breaks into a grin. She looks like a jailhouse version of Ms. Frizzle from *The Magic School Bus.*

"Here, let me help you." She takes the box of books that I have pilfered from my own collection to feed my starving classroom bookcase. "You're Hannah? The new teacher? I'm Yvonne, the science teacher. You will be fine. Just breathe, stay calm, and don't let them bully you." She says this last part laughingly, but doesn't add anything about joking.

"Who is 'them'?"

"The kids. Well, mostly the kids. The probation staff, too. And some of the education staff." She lowers her voice a bit, leaning into me. She smells of violets and coffee.

"So trust no one, pretty much."

"Oh I wouldn't say that. Some of us are all right. Have you met the new boss yet? How is she?" Yvonne dumps my things onto a long conference table in the middle of the break room, surrounded by mismatched chairs. There are three large windows looking out onto the sloping hill and the road that it runs down to. One whole wall is taken up by the fridge, a long gray counter, and a small steel sink. Lunch bags and coffee mugs are scattered about, a ravaged box of bagels shoved to the side. Three white boards fill the spaces between the windows.

"You haven't met your own boss? The hell kind of ghost ship am I on, anyways?"

"Not this one. There is a new one every year. Five principals in five years." She shuffles a stack of last month's magazines and stained fliers on a side table, arranging them into a sad pile of paper no one wants to read or dispose of.

"They all leave after one year?" Was this wisdom or cowardice? Sometimes they wear the same clothes.

"This isn't the easiest place to work," Yvonne smiles sadly and hands me a cup of tea, the tendrils of mint stinging my eyes.

We walk into the sallyport together to cross over into the school department. "Do you know about this population?" Yvonne shifts my box of books from one arm to another, two bags of her own hanging from her hand. Out of one hangs a plastic baby doll with a dented head, arm raised in a jovial salute.

"A tiny bit. I used to volunteer with kids in jail."

"Just remember that you are going to have kids of all ages and grade levels and ability levels in one class. Some kids may be in eighth grade, some may be in eleventh grade. And the eighth grader might be a better reader and writer than the eleventh grader. You will have Nortenos for the first period, then the girls, then Surenos. The schedule rotates, too."

"Nikki mentioned that the other day. Does that actually work? Having kids from ninth and eleventh grade in the same class?"

The door buzzes and Yvonne pushes it open with her shoulder. I realize that I am too nervous about what today will be like to be anxious about being stuck in the sallyport. Maybe this is the thing to do; find something else to freak out about to distract yourself from what actually frightens you.

"It's less problematic. They used to mix the groups, but there were too many fights. So now they separate them by gang. " Yvonne sees me to my classroom door, using her key to unlock it. "Don't worry too much. Always count the pencils. They will try to steal them. And I keep chocolate in my desk. I suggest you do the same."

"For the kids?"

"Oh no. We can't feed them." Yvonne shakes her head very quickly.

"Sounds like a zoo." Even as a kid, I found zoos depressing and unnatural. And yet, here I am.

"It has its similarities. But seriously keep some chocolate in your desk. There will be days when you need it. My classroom is the last one at the end of the hall before the bathrooms. Just yell if you need help."

I hit the lights and pull out the metaphor and simile worksheets for today. It's a very comfortable topic and one that will help me gauge where each of my kids are in terms of figurative language. My paltry contribution of books takes up half of one of the ten shelves in it: Anne Sexton, David Sedaris, biographies on North Korean defectors, everything Anthony Bourdain had ever written. This is what little criminals read, right?

As the clock ticks down to 8:30, chatter begins to swell in the hallway. The teachers are gathered at the glass wall facing the field and the housing units, making small talk with one another and periodically glancing outwards, anxiously awaiting the student's procession to school. Aside from Yvonne and Sara, there are two other teachers I have not met before. One is a tall, older man with thinning blond hair and tired, wise eyes. He holds a plastic coffee thermos and listens more than he speaks. The other is shorter and a bit younger. He has thick black hair and is eating yogurt and fruit out of a paper cup.

"Ralph and Jack, this is Hannah, the new English teacher," Yvonne calls over her shoulder at the group as she tapes up water conservation posters.

"Nice to meet you. I'm the History teacher," Jack grins, shaking my hand. His hair is flecked with gray, like a haphazardly tinseled Christmas tree. Sunglasses hang around his neck, catching the bits of fruit that fall from his spoon.

Ralph gives me a tight-lipped smile. He seems like a guy of few words. His long sleeve, button-down shirt and dress slacks combined with his sneakers make him look like he has a job interview to go to, but he is planning on running there. "First teaching job?"

"Yea. Kind of nervous. Well, not kind of. Really nervous. Terrified actually." If that stunning endorsement doesn't make my new colleagues respect me, I don't know what will.

"Oh, you will be fine. The nervousness goes away," Jack says.

"Or you just get used to being nervous all the time," chuckles Yvonne.

Everyone casts their eyes back towards the units. There is a moment of quiet. I realize that I have been clenching my jaw this whole time. *I have confidence in confidence alone.*

Then out of the mist appears a guard in all black, followed by twenty or so young men. Clad in dark blue pants and sweatshirts, they walk in a single file line, their hands clasped behind their backs. They stare straight ahead, vigilant and orderly as military cadets. Jack and Yvonne return to their rooms, leaving Ralph and I standing there, gazing out at the approaching procession. It's the world's most somber parade.

"Whose group is that? Are those my kids?"

"Those are everyone's kids. Each class will have kids from each housing unit in it. Except for the girls. They stay together. But for the four other periods, you will have a mixture of boys in blue, green, purple, and yellow."

The blue group splits at the door, some being escorted to science or history or my class. They seem to know where to go. They are already one step ahead of me. Two young men approach my classroom, arms still tucked behind them.

"Good morning, gentlemen." I am smiling so hard at them, I look like an insane person.

"You the new teacher?" A Latino boy with jet black eyes and beautiful, wavy hair down to his shoulders eyes me skeptically. His handsome poker face is a wall covered in signs written in a foreign language. He is thickly muscular and heavily tattooed, faded images spanning his arms and neck. The other boy standing a foot or so behind him is a bit taller and much thinner, also a dark-eyed Latino.

"That I am." I try to think of something humorous to say to break the ice, but my mind is a desert right now, tumbleweeds skittering across the horizon.

The boys nod and saunter into the room, sliding into adjacent seats in the corner of the room farthest from me. Their eyes jump from corner to corner, frisking the windows and doorways, scrutinizing them for threats, for weaknesses.

The roll sheet has a housing unit next to each student's name. Because they are in blue, I am able to find one of their names. "Jose?"

"Yep," says the enigmatic young John Leguizamo.

"I am sorry...I don't see your name on here." The roll sheet lists only Jose as being in blue.

"Carlos." The other boy flicks his chin up in way of response. His cheekbones are so sharp, his eyes large and hazel. His hair is in a long, thick braid that reaches almost to his waist. There are four small dots tattooed in a diamond pattern beneath his left eye.

I find a Carlos, but it is listed as living in the green unit even though he is wearing a blue sweatshirt. "I see your name, but it says you live in another place."

"They moved me." Carlos rolls his eyes, irritated that he has to explain this to me.

"You went to court?" Jose puts his foot up on the desk in front of him.

"They played me, blood! One year. Pinche puta D.A. I'ma smoke that fucker when I get out." Carlos punches his open palm, casting an eye at me.

"Well it's so nice to meet you!"

They both look at me like I am a meal they did not order. They begin to speak only in low, hushed Spanish. There is a new procession of kids heading down, the boys in green. I straddle the doorway, keeping one eye on the students in my classroom and watching the boys in green sweatshirts approach. Five boys turn towards my classroom without breaking their stride. I ask for their names at the doorway like a bouncer for the world's most unexciting club.

"Juan." His intense, almond-shaped eyes are cautiously reading me. His hair, like Carlos, is also in a long thick braid nearly down to his waist. He is thicker and shorter than Carlos, with chapped, split lips.

"Kevin." He flips his long, black hair out of his brown eyes. His shoulders are hunched forward a bit and his lip curls a bit when he says his name.

"Eduardo." The smallest and palest of the four, his hair hanging in greasy clumps around his enormous head. His brown eyes are enormous, almost doll-like. His features are delicate and slightly feminine. He eyes me nervously and picks at his fingernails.

"Antonio." His hair is a giant frizzy halo around his head. He is mixed, Latino and black, with pale hazel eyes and pockmarks dotting his beautiful face. He cracks a grin as I desperately scan the roll sheet for his name. He points at it, grinning, "That's me right there."

"Jorge." There is a line of stitches across his thick right eyebrow and scratch marks on his face and neck. His voice is a deep baritone with a hint of Spanish. He rolls his r and runs a hand over his buzzed head. He is built like a tank, and walks with his large fists balled at his sides.

"Can you do this inside? I can't have them standing out in the hall like this." The guard that walked them down is standing there with his hands on his hips. He is portly and short, with a radio and handcuffs on his belt. It's the same guy who waved at Sara while she was giving me the tour.

"Sorry. I just wanted to get their names."

"Well, do it inside. Please." The pleasantry is an afterthought.

"Okay. Sorry. What's your name?" This is less out of curiosity and more out of a need to know what to yell if something turns ugly.

"Mr. Thompson," he says gruffly. No first names for any adult here, apparently. "You replacing the dead lady?"

"Yea. I'm Miss Wehr."

"Good luck." He sinks into a rolling chair he has dragged over to the doorway and cracks open a crossword puzzle book.

The boys take their seats, slapping hands and greeting Carlos and Jose. Everyone seems to know everyone. I guess I can ditch the whole introduction game I was going to start class off with. *I must dream of the things I am seeking/ I am seeking the courage I lack.*

I take a deep breath and step to the front of the room. This is curtain rise on a nine month long play. "Good morning, gentlemen." The forced school portrait smile clashes with churning waves of terror in my gut. I feel like a mismatched pair of shoes.

A light skinned Latino boy with a lip mark tattoo on his neck and a black eye walks in, drowning in an oversized purple sweatshirt. Head down, he sits in the desk closest to the door, not making eye contact. Carlos and Juan whisper something to each other.

I am back to the roll sheet, trying to match the color with the boy. "Marco? Nice to meet you. I'm Miss Wehr."

"Eh." His upper lip spasms, a sullen acknowledgment.

"Well, let's try this again. Good mor..."

Another tall, lanky boy with in a yellow shirt comes in. His head is completely shaved, except for a ponytail coming out of the back of his head. His skin is a beautiful raw umber and he is almost a whole head taller than the rest of the boys.

"What the fuck you doin' here, Jesus?" Carlos yells across the room to one of the boys. Jesus throws his hands up and grins, revealing a missing front tooth.

"Ummm...can we not cuss in class?" I feel like I am already asking too much.

"I will try. Teacher." Carlos rolls his eyes.

"Third time's the charm, I guess. Good morning, guys!"

Jose turns to say something to Kevin, and the rest stare at me. Jorge spins his desk towards Juan.

"Where's Mrs. Lee?" asks Jesus. Considering that he was here when the last teacher was here, yet did not know that she had passed away in the room, means that he has been in, out, and back in again within the last month.

"You didn't hear, blood?" Kevin asks. Blood. The nickname used between fellow Nortenos.

"Nah, man. What happened?" Kevin and Jesus's conversation jumps back and forth across the classroom like an indecisive toad, arcing the heads of the other boys who are silently staring at me.

"She died, blood." There is no sympathy or sadness in Kevin's voice, just a simple recitation of fact, like multiplication tables.

"So you're our new teacher?" Jesus turns to me, incredulous and slightly amused.

"Yes. And please do not call each other blood."

Jesus' eyebrows go up, a quiet challenge. This is a moment of truth. "Nah, it ain't like that. Blood just means that you are a friend." He gives me a smile that has nothing to do with happiness.

"I know what blood means."

Jesus does jazz hands.

"Did you look up gang slang on Wikipedia or something?" Antonio grins, putting his feet up on the empty desk in front of him.

"I did some research, yes."

"Yea? And what you find out?" Jose narrows his eyes at me.

"Probably nothing that you don't already know yourself." I feel like a grilling slab of meat.

"Why? You think I'm a gang member? Just cause I'm Latino, I must be a gang member?" The other boys are grinning at Jose, enjoying this game. They look amused, but Jose looks serious. I get the feeling that everyone who meets him probably assumes that he is a gang member.

"I'm sorry, I didn't mean to imply..."

"Racist! That's what that is! It's racist!" Jesus jabs his long bony finger at me, leaning so far forward in his desk that it rocks forward. He slams his feet down, harder than necessary to stop the desk from tipping. I flinch at the noise and his grin gets even bigger. That anxious feeling begins to envelop me. My heart starts to break dance and my face burns. This is not how this is supposed to go.

"Do you want to go back to your room?" I stammer, in a voice that is anything but authoritative. Wow. Three minutes into my first class and I have already resorted to threatening.

There is a moment of awkward silence, the rest of the boys watching us both, waiting to see who will back down first. Jesus finally nods, almost imperceptibly and leans back into his chair. This is below him and he will not dignify this with his attention anymore. The rest of the boys resume talking softly to one another. I am already disappointed in myself. I feel challenged and I immediately jump right to threatening? The hell kind of classroom management is that?

I set down my clipboard and stand silently in front of the class, waiting for them to stop murmuring to each other. This tactic worked like a charm at the school that I did my student teaching at last year. Then again those were highly regimented honor students, not fifteen-year-old armed robbers. They keep talking, scooting their desks closer to each other. A few glance at me, shrug at my silence, and resume their conversations. Subtlety is not going to work with this group. "Gentlemen, I would like to begin by telling you about myself."

They quiet down, turning expectantly towards me with looks that say, 'you have three seconds to engage me'. This is a like the worst parts of open mic night and the best parts of a firing squad in one solitary experience.

"I am from Southern California." I should have known better than to start with that.

"Fuck scraps," Carlos mutters.

"What's a scrap?" I am so lost. From the doorway, Mr. Thompson snorts and shakes his head. His eyes are glued to his iPhone so either I just made a big misstep or Angry Birds is particularly amusing today.

"So you've never seen a Northerner?" Kevin asks, mischief sparkling in his large brown eyes.

"I am new to the area, yes." There are so many land-minds here. It suddenly occurs to me that the only thing separating me from real bodily harm is a desk and Mr. Thompson, who is texting at the moment.

Carlos raises his eyebrows, glances around for affirmation, and grins, "Just remember you ain't in Southern Cali no more. This here is our neighborhood."

"You aren't in your neighborhood anymore. You are in a classroom which makes this my neighborhood." My hands are clammy and my heart is slamming against my chest like even it's trying to get out of here. Where is this ground-standing coming from? A smarter person would not be taunting the sharks whose tank they had just jumped into. There is a series of giggles from the boys as they grin and elbow each other, watching to see who will win. If I dig my nails into my palms any harder, I am going to look like the poster child for spontaneous stigmata.

"Teacher, you don't know where you are at." This is Custer's last stand. Or rather Carlos's.

"I know exactly where I am at: my classroom. So leave your neighborhood at the door or get out." Thankfully the table in front of me hides my trembling legs.

Mr. Thompson looks up from his phone, a slightly bemused expression on his weatherworn face. There is a moment of quiet and Carlos finally drops his eyes to his desk. Teacher 1, student 0. I am white-knuckling the desk. Kevin smirks, shaking his head.

"Moving on. I want to start today with an exercise on similes and metaphors. For some of you this will be new, for some of you it will be review. I apologize to those of you for whom this will be too easy. I just need to get a baseline on where you are all at, since this is the first time I am meeting you." I weave my way up and down the aisles, stepping over long spider legs threading the spaces between the desks. Only Eduardo tucks his feet in as I walk past, but the swiftness with which he does it is more out of a self-protective reflex than courtesy. Jesus brushes his worksheet off his desk. Stupidly, I bend over to pick it up. Someone slaps their hands together. There is a rush of giggles as I snap up so quickly that my lower back spasms for a moment. Lesson learned: no bending over.

"Very cute," I tell Jesus, slapping the paper on his desk.

"I don't know what you mean. Teacher."

"Grab a partner. You can work together."

Carlos grabs Kevin in a headlock, almost falling out of his desk. Kevin begins to swing wildly at Carlos, his flailing arms a windmill of frustration.

"Knock it off, " Mr. Thompson says loudly and robotically, still looking at his phone.

"You said grab a partner. Teacher." Carlos is a jailhouse Cheshire Cat.

"You smell like shit. Dirty ass motherfucker," Kevin grumbles, smoothing his hair back into place.

The boys pair up to work on the paper. I walk around, answering questions and assisting struggling students. This is the teaching that I was trained for: teach, assign, help. It's a formula that is pounded into every new teacher before they leave graduate school. It assumes that students learn the same way and at the same pace. It's not a strategy I plan on using every day, but I have to get some sort of reading on where the kids are at academically, what they do and don't know. These kids didn't get arrested with their transcripts and STAR scores in their back pockets, so what each kid can and can't do is a total mystery to me. Hell, I don't even know what grade any of these kids are in or when they actually attended school last.

Jesus and Carlos are giggling over their paper, never a good sign on such a boring assignment as this. I slide up alongside and read the simile that they had to complete over their shoulders: 'Skinny as a...tweaker bitch.'

"That is not appropriate."

"But it's true. Tweaker bitches are skinny as fuck." Carlos explains this like he is telling a five-year-old how rain works.

"Erase it, rewrite it, and watch your mouth. This is a school, not a barrio."

Jorge is drawing the laugh now, cry later faces on his paper. "We are done," he says snatching up both papers and shoving them at my chest.

I lean down halfway before catching myself and dropping into a seat, "Right here you said this was a metaphor. But you see how it says 'like' right there? That makes it a simile." Their silence makes me realize how condescending my tone is.

"We aren't retards, you know. Just cause we are in here, that doesn't mean we are stupid," Jorge sneers. His irritation reads like tree rings; he has always been thought of as stupid because of his choices.

"I'm so sorry. I didn't mean to talk to you like you are younger than you are."

"It's okay, " Juan says, his tone slightly softer than before. "You are new."

"Thank you. I am still learning you guys, the same way I guess you are learning me."

"Speaking of learning," Antonio holds up the paper that he has impaled on his pencil. "I don't see how this is gonna help me in life."

Shit, he has a good point. How does this help anyone in life? Whose life was ever saved by a simile? "Well, I suppose that understanding figurative language makes it easier to read." Even as I am saying this, I realize it sounds like a piss-poor excuse. Certainly wouldn't have motivated me when I was their age.

"We don't read," Jorge flatlines. He speaks for the group apparently. None of the boys object.

"Do you want to go to college?" I am grasping at straws here.

"Nope." He is enjoying this, this being obstinate. Being difficult was one of my favorite teenage pastimes, too.

"What do you want to do?" Yes and no questions are not going to give me the upper hand here.

"Make money." His face goes hard and flat as a table.

"All jobs require you to be able to read and write. This is just helping you strengthen your skills."

"I don't need to read and write to make money. I already make money without it."

"What job doesn't require you to at least be able to write

and read a little?" I know the answer already.

"Slanging dope," he grins, throwing his worksheet that he had fashioned into a paper airplane as we were talking. It takes a nosedive into the trashcan.

At the doorway, Mr. Thompson stands up and announces that it is time for the boys to move to their next class. I am floundering for a reason to give him as to why figurative language is important, but nothing is coming to mind. As the boys file out, Jesus calls over his shoulder, "Nice try, though. Teacher."

All those children, they will look up to me and mind me with each step/ I am most certain.

September 12

The boys straggle in, with all the grace and uniformity of a gaggle of feral cats, leapfrogging over desks as they clamor to their seats. The staff member that has accompanied this group is small and portly, a middle-aged Latino man with glasses and a gold chain peeking out from the neckline of his black sweatshirt.

"Miss Wehr," I smile, holding out my hand.

"Mr. Robbins," he grins, shaking my hand. "How you holding up?"

"Not bad. Trying to just get a feel for everything and everyone."

"You'll do fine. This is your Norteno class, so if you see...HEY! Jesus, what's your problem?"

I didn't even notice that there was a problem. But somehow during the five seconds I have been talking to Mr. Robbins, two kids are squaring off over a seat in the corner.

"There's no problem if he gets outta my seat!" Jesus is pointing at Eduardo in the corner of the classroom.

"Did you pay for that chair? No? That's right! That's not your goddamn seat, that's the county's. So sit somewhere else and shut up."

Jesus stomps to a desk at the other side of the room and throws himself into it, sulking and shooting hateful glances at Eduardo who is deliberately not looking at him.

"Thank you for that," I hiss to Mr. Robbins. "I didn't even notice anything was wrong."

"First one's free, kid," Mr. Robbins grins, settling into the same chair that Mr. Thompson sat in yesterday. "But you have to see everything. Turning your back like that, that's how fights start." Even as he is talking, his eyes never meet mine. They flicker between the boys, spastic as sputtering bulb.

"Thanks for the heads up." Three minutes into class and I have already dropped the ball. Walking back to the front of the room, I ask the boys to simmer down.

"Geez, lady. That how you treat your friends? You tell them

to settle down and be quiet?" Jesus grins.

"My friends don't generally have to be told to quit crawling over desks."

"Well, then you need more exciting friends. What your name again? Miss Weird?"

"Wehr. No 'd'."

"Can I call you Miss Weird?" His eyebrows arch playfully. He is testing the waters, a dolphin throwing out sonar to see where the obstacles are up ahead.

I have to be a giant, immovable rock right now. "Can I call you Janet? No? Well then, same goes."

We discuss similes and their sister, the metaphor. About half the boys know what I am talking about, the other half say that they understand but their worried expressions betray them. They do not know what the hell I am talking about, but they refuse to admit that.

Eduardo, the bird-like boy who took Jesus's seat, raises his hand for help. He has delicate, Elfish features and worried brown eyes. I am momentarily stunned by his manners.

"I don't get this word," he says, revealing a mouth full of cracked and jagged teeth. There are a few kids who are in desperate need of a visit to the dentist. Their gang must not offer good dental insurance. "What does 'gentle' mean?"

"Yea, I didn't get that one either." Antonio leans into our conversation from the other side of the room. His hazel eyes glitter and glow, partially obscured by his unkempt, curly hair. One of his upper teeth is turned at an angle like a fang and it catches on his bottom lip when he closes his mouth. This is so much more than a vocabulary question.

"Does anyone else not know what gentle means?" I ask the class.

"I don't either," says Jesus, who is re-braiding his long hair, his thin fingers working nimbly and swiftly. He could almost pass as Native American with his high cheekbones, fierce countenance, and intense black eyes.

I explain gentle the only way I know how. I tell him it is how you touch something that is very valuable and fragile. They blink at me and I realize that they have never done this. "It's the opposite of rough or violent." Their faces light up with understanding.

Jorge's arms are folded in defiance, his pencil lying idle on the desk. His jaw pulsates as he clenches his teeth rapidly, like a heartbeat. "I'm done. This shit is hella easy."

"Really? That's great!"

"Well, it's not rocket surgery." He rolls his eyes at my stupidity.

"No, no it is definitely not that."

"Can you believe that?" I ask Yvonne during lunch. "He didn't know what gentle means." Our small lunchroom has fifteen people crammed around one long table, like a really rushed Thanksgiving where everyone brings their own meal. There is one microwave and a fridge that is way too small to accommodate the breakfasts, snacks, and lunches of fifteen people. The energy is so hectic in the break-room: the rush to get your food out, wait for the microwave, heat it, shovel it into your face, grab your attendance sheet from the secretary and make it back through the sallyport and into your classroom before your students do. You never know how long you are going to be in the sallyport, going either direction or when exactly the staff will bring the kids to school, so our thirty-five minute lunch is usually about twenty minutes. There is no bell system, so the kids are brought down by the guards at their whim. This could be five minutes early or twenty minutes late.

"Yes, I can." She shovels salad from her plate onto mine, strips of red pepper and crumbling goat cheese falling into the space between us. "You have to remember that a lot of these kids have a long history of truancy. Some started skipping school in the third grade. So there are going to be huge gaps in their knowledge. Things that we would assume a sixteen year old would know, they may not know."

"It's like trying to pour water into a Swiss cheese," adds Jack from the other side of the table.

"Exactly. You can't expect to teach them everything or even get them up to grade level. They just have too much knowledge missing. And you may only have them for a week. It's best to set a reasonable goal for yourself," Yvonne sighs. "Just teach them anything. Even if it's one thing, it's one thing more than they knew before they came to your class."

"Or just try to get through a day without a fight," Jack grins.

"You can't save them from themselves," Yvonne says.

Driving home that first night, my mind attempts to conjure up a world in which gentle does not exist. A place where gentle has no home. Where gentle is as foreign a concept as nuclear physics. Gentle is a country never lived in. This is opposite world and not in a singing flowers, *Alice in Wonderland* type of way. This is a world where rough is a way of life, where the fragile are crushed underfoot and what cannot withstand severe hardships and brutality is buried and forgotten. I pass a sign on the freeway: East Palo Alto.

September 20

My student's previous relationship to writing is unknown to me. I find myself envious of teachers in the average high school who at the very least receive their new brood of kids each year with a basic understanding of what they can and can't do. There are transcripts, test scores, some medical paperwork to at least let you know if the student needs glasses or has been vaccinated for chicken pox. If nothing else, they at least know that if the kid is entering their class, it's a pretty good indicator that they completed the previous grade.

I mentioned to Yvonne that I was having a hard time finding any academic or behavioral testing results on Eduardo and she asked me how many kids I know that keep a copy of their transcripts in their back pockets while they were living under a bridge and prostituting themselves for meth.

This is teaching without a net. Thankfully, my students can communicate well verbally and they process information swiftly. No matter where my kids were living before, whether in a condo with parents or in a car with a drug dealer, communicating verbally was necessary. Writing isn't practiced nearly as much outside of the classroom, for any kid. A junior higher on summer break could go for months without writing anything even close to an essay. So while most students practice verbal communication skills consistently and unconsciously, their writing wheels can rust much sooner.

The air is thin and static today, everyone stretched taut and trembling like a rubber band. The institution is a belt pulled a few notches tighter. Gang tension, Yvonne says. It seems a vague, yet insidious term. How do you prove tension? If there was physical proof, that would just be aggression, right? As it stands, there is only the threat of something which is often more frightening than the thing itself. A whole institution as a bully big brother standing with his hand inches from your face, saying he is not really going to hit you.

"Gang tension varies," Yvonne says, dragging a stroller containing a plastic preemie doll across her classroom. She teaches sex education a lot more than the average high school teacher because of the amount of teen mothers and fathers we have in here. Out of the nine boys in my first period class, five of them are already fathers and two of them have multiple kids. "The staff may be finding more communication between the boys, or they could have found a weapon. Maybe the boys are planning an attack. It's different every time, but you can always feel it."

The students were clearly feeling it too, their movements a bit jerkier, legs bouncing under desks, fingers tapping out telegraphs no one will read. A classroom of marionettes in the hands of amateurs.

"You still here?" Carlos glares at me.

"No, I'm not."

The chatter of the boys and Mr. Thompson's radio quiet for a moment, leaving only the gravel grace of Louis Armstrong rising from the CD player. The boys look momentarily confused, then offended.

"What the hell is this music?" Jesus asks, pointing accusatorially.

"It's Satchmo! Isn't he wonderful?"

"I don't care what his gang name is; he needs a fucking cough drop."

Taking this more personally than I should (last I checked Louis and I were not related), I stomp to the CD player and smack it open, filling the room with silence. "That better?"

"Don't get butt-hurt. It just sounds like elevator music," Carlos grins.

"It is not elevator music! It's classic! Timeless!"

"Well, if teaching doesn't work out, you can be a DJ," Jesus says. "You can be a DJ in an elevator. That way people would have to listen to it."

"Lord. Anyways, today we are going to try our hand at writing." How I expect to engage anyone with a flimsy line like that is beyond me.

"How do you try a hand?" Jesus is already running out of patience with me.

"It's a saying. It means to give something a shot."

Kevin turns back to Juan, saying, "Oh you know who got shot last weekend?"

"We are not talking about that right now." God, these kids are going to drive me insane and it's only half an hour in on my tenth day of work.

"Well, when am I supposed to talk about it?" Kevin swivels back, narrowing his eyes at me.

"I don't know! Just not now." Homicide discussions seem more suited to PE class.

Kevin rolls his eyes and fixes his gaze on the wall, which is apparently more pleasing and interesting than I am. Fantastic.

"Try your hand is an example of figurative language called an idiom. An example would be an eye for eye which means to get back at someone the same way they hurt you. Like if I took your French fries and you stole mine to get back at me."

Antonio who has stretched his legs through two rows of desks, leaving so little of his torso in his seat that he looks seconds away from sliding out of it says, "I would just upgrade and take the whole potato."

"You have friends that carry potatoes around with them?"

"What are we gonna write about?" Juan asks, giving me his sideways skeptical glance. None of the kids trust me yet, but he is working overtime to make sure I know this. "Cause honestly, there's nothing I want to share with you."

"That's fair. You don't know me, so you have no reason to trust me."

"Uhh…yea. That's okay?" Juan looks confused and a little unsteady, like a dog trying to stand in a moving car.

"Sure. I wouldn't want to share something personal with someone I don't know." This is like circling a bull. One step forward, flash of cape, two steps back. "How about a topic that isn't too personal? Social issues? Current events? Virtues?"

"What's a virtue?" Jose breaks the sullen silence he has managed to maintain throughout the period.

"It's a positive character trait, like honesty or compassion or respect."

"Respect. Respect is everything." Jorge nods slowly as he speaks, the rest of the boys turning into slow-motion Bobble head dolls. The cape has been lunged for. Now all I have to do is not make them feel they are being lured into a trap. I feel like one of those creepy men by the park, trying to entice kids into his van with sweets. But I don't even have candy bars here, just pencils.

"Let's talk about that for a second. Respect is important. But is it more important to be respected or to be feared?" This topic must split like a fault line; in order for there to be discussion, there has to be discord.

The boys turn to one another to discuss before proffering their opinions. Most of them felt that respect was paramount and the few that looked like they disagreed are holding their tongues. Being of one mind seems pretty important around here.

"Respect is everything," Jesus speaks for the group. "If you don't have respect, you have nothing. People don't respect you, they are going to play you. Respect is your name and your heart and your blood."

"So how do you get respect?" The cape blowing in the breeze, hot dirt rising up as the bull squares off.

In lieu of crickets, there is the static of Mr. Thompson's radio. He sits in the doorway with his sunglasses still on. He is either hung-over or far and away the coolest person in the room.

"You have to make people respect you," Juan says slowly. "You have to be a man of your word, handle your responsibilities, and take care of your family. You have to make people fear you too, though. They have to know you don't take no disrespect."

"Is there a difference between fearing someone and respecting them?" A ripple of red through the dust, temptation warning of its own potential.

A cacophony of yes and no rose quickly and fell silent just as fast. Confused, the boys look to one another for an explanation for the fracture, each head of the hydra suddenly realizing that their brain was not mutual. This is our moment of truth.

"Why don't you write down why your opinion is the right one?"

The boys glance at one another, unsure who will charge first. A silence settles on the class, a hot hush of anticipation. There is nothing in the world of this arena but me with my cape, begging them to believe that I will not hurt them for their trust and the collective apprehensive beast of them.

Juan finally speaks, his mouth the first hoof-fall towards me, "Gimme some fucking paper."

September 22

In a regular high school there are passing periods between each class; a precious few moments for a teacher to breath and use the bathroom. A grace period as the kids straggle to Biology or World History. In juvie, the kids are led directly from one class to the next in a straight, silent line. As all of the classrooms are only a few feet apart, smashed into one corridor, it takes the kids less than a minute to switch classrooms. But in those sixty seconds there is more than enough to keep you occupied. Check that all the pencils have been returned. Check that they are all about the same height. If one is noticeably shorter, it means that it has been snapped and stored in a kid's sock. Check that the metal bit that attaches each eraser to the pencil is still in tact. Check under each desk for hidden weapons and notes. Check for tagging on desks and books.

If someone didn't have OCD before working here, they certainly would now. As I crawl between the rows of desks on my hands and knees, checking beneath each one for contraband, I can't help but wonder what came first: the sneakiness or the suspicion. If someone was always thinking the worst of me, always expecting me to be deceitful, never trusting me, then I might be more inclined to live down to the precedent that was set for me. There is a murmur of voices at my door and manage to pull myself up with all the grace of an octopus falling out of a tree as the boys saunter in.

"Why were you on the floor?" smiles Jose as he settles into a front row seat. He looks like a toothpaste commercial for convicts. "Were you checking for kites?"

"Kites? Why would there be a kite in here?" I need a translator. Even words wear different clothes inside the hall.

"A kite. A note. Or a shiv."

"It's hella shady. Nobody trusts us!" Jose angrily kicks the desk in front of him.

"Look where you are at," Antonio laughs. "You think anyone trusts kids in jail? That's why we are here. They don't even trust us with freedom."

"Yea, but everybody thinks the worst of us. Like we have no honor. Like everything we do is evil."

"Nobody believes the guilty, son." Antonio smiles sadly.

"Not even just in here," says Jose. " Mexicans are always in trouble with someone, even when we didn't do anything wrong."

Juan and Jesus straggle in from the computer lab where they had been doing academic placement testing which is humorous since we only have one class for each subject. It's not like a gifted kid can be moved from English to AP English.

They notice the sullen mood instantly and take their seats swiftly and silently. The way these kids pick up nuances and shifts in tone or mood is amazing. Eduardo trails in quietly behind them. He casts a worried look at me and takes a seat in the front row.

"I understand how it feels to not be trusted. When I was a teenager, my parents didn't trust me either. It really hurt. I felt like no matter what I did to show them I was being honest, they didn't believe me." I am holding my hands out to them, like I could offer them anything they needed. Like anyone could.

"How do you make someone trust you?" asks Antonio.

"My mom said she wouldn't trust me ever again. She said I had lied to her too many times," Jose whispers, gazing at his feet.

"My mom, too. She said she won't even come get me when I get released," Juan says. "I screwed up too many times."

"I think there are a lot of things in our lives that we don't like. But there are also a lot of good things. Maybe that's what we should write about: the things we are grateful for. Can you guys write a list of things you are happy about? It can be big or small things, just anything that comes to mind."

"Gotta stay positive. That's what my therapist says. Gotta stay positive," nods Antonio.

The boys begin to write quietly. I sit in the peace of the moment, feeling my face glowing. What wonderful boys I have. I have reached them. Nothing will ever go wrong again. Wait... Jesus is not writing.

"What are you thankful for?"

"Nothing."

"There is nothing good in your life? Your family? Your friends? Your school?"

"My mom doesn't want anything to do with me any more. She is scared to have me at home around the little kids. My grandma doesn't want nothing more to do with me. My pops peaced out when I was a baby. None of my friends have been writing me and my school told me I can't come back. Nobody in my life wants me." He clips off each bullet point in this litany with a bitterness that wants no consolation, no assistance. He is merely explaining each brick that composes the wall between us.

"You woke up this morning. Lot of people in the world didn't. You may not have woken up in a place you wanted to be in, but at least you are alive. You walked to class. No one had to push you in a wheelchair. You can hear the words coming out of my mouth. " This last one is not a strong point to end on.

Jesus narrows his eyes at me, mouth turning up in a sneer. He scans the classroom and his eyes rest on Eduardo. "I am grateful that I don't look like a tweaker monkey like that motherfucker right there."

Eduardo's head doesn't rise but his bottom lip begins to tremble. I am shocked into silence for a second. Then my anger snaps back like a boomerang. "Get. Out. Now."

"What?" Jesus smiles up at me.

I rise to my feet. At the doorway Mr. Robbins does the same.

"I was just playing! Come on now! I was just joking! He knows that! " His eyes go big and he is starting to get worried.

"Shouldn't you make a beeping sound when you back up like that?" I snarl, all decorum evaporated.

"I didn't do nothing!" Jesus snarls at me, eyes narrowing.

"It ain't an option! Get your ass out here!" Mr. Robbins is making his way across the classroom.

"This is bullshit!" Jesus is clenching his desk, knuckles white with rage. He looks about two seconds away from jumping over the desk and wrapping his fingers around my neck. The other boys glance nervously at the guards who have started pouring into the classroom.

"Get the hell up now, Jesus!" Mr. Robbins lumbers towards him, ready to drag him from his seat. Jesus rises slowly, tilting his chin back until his eyes are barely visible on the horizon of his face.

I take a step away from him as he passes by, spitting, "Fuck this shit."

Mr. Robbins escorts him out of the room, murmuring sternly into his ear. There is a moment of quiet in the classroom. The younger boys look at me, wide-eyed. The older boys lower their heads, refusing to make eye contact with me. I have shamed Jesus in front of the homies. This is not okay.

They return to their writing, glancing cautiously up at me every minute or so. They are waiting to get in trouble, too. The adults they are used to dealing with must cast a wide net of anger and anyone in the vicinity gets caught, regardless if they did anything wrong or not. When I pass by Eduardo's desk, he pulls his head into his shoulders slightly as if he is expecting a blow.

I come to a stop by Carlos's desk. On his paper, in crude Roman numerals is XIV. The fourteenth letter of the alphabet is N, the most loved letter of Nuestra Familia. I snatch the paper from his desk, my tide of rage returning to shore. I march to the door, stick my head out and signal for Mr. Robbins who seems to have wandered away.

"What? You said write about what's good in your life! My gang is good!"

"I was born at night, but not last night. Don't play, Carlos. Your insolence is going to cause you problems in life."

"My what?"

"Insolence! Your insolence!" Saying the same unknown word over and over again doesn't help anyone understand it any better, but I am so pissed off I can't think of anything else to say.

"My uncle has to take insolence. He has diabetes," Antonio adds helpfully.

Carlos protests until Mr. Robbins barks from the doorway for him to get off his ass. He angrily stomps to the door. At this point I feel like the world's most horrible teacher. I have had to dismiss two students in as many minutes. Does this mean that I am losing control? Nothing is going right. I have failed. I am a horrible teacher.

And all these children will look up to me and mind me with each step. Godammit, Julie Andrews.

At lunch, I lay my head down on the table beside my microwavable quiche. Everything feels so temporary, transient. Most of the people I work with don't know my full name. I am living in a hotel. I don't have a washer or dryer so I had to go to the laundromat yesterday where two loads of my whites were stolen out of their dryers while I was next door getting a sandwich. The air conditioning wasn't working last night, so I sweated myself to sleep. My whole life feels like an adjustment, an existence on a hinge.

"You okay?" Yvonne smiles at me as she chops tomatoes into her salad.

I barely know this lady and I adore her. Any shred of sanity that I am managing to maintain throughout all of this is due mostly to her support and compassion. "I had to kick out two kids. I just feel bad about it."

"I used to feel badly about it, too. But you need to look at it this way; we are teaching them how to behave. Most of these kids have not been in school in years. They need to be taught how to behave in class." She takes a seat beside me, shoveling half of her fruit salad onto my plate. "We are not just teaching young people, we are showing them how to behave. If our students are going to succeed in the outside world, they need to understand what is and is not appropriate behavior. Otherwise there is no chance of them maintaining a job or a healthy relationship."

This woman is right. This woman is absolutely right. Thank God for this woman and her wisdom and her salads.

My period following lunch today is the girl's class. I am still trying to gain footing with this group. They are a messy and hurt lot, but lovable and endearing despite their sloppy attempts at gangster behavior. It is a small class, only a handful of girls. The number of male students dwarfs the amount of female students ten to one. They murmur their greetings, sliding lazily into their seats, full and sleepy from lunch.

"Today we are going to do some writing about the concept of home and community. What makes something home for us? What makes us feel a part of a larger group?"

Shawna, a stunning seventeen-year-old girl with a striking resemblance to Iman, is sucking her thumb. I open my mouth to mention that this is not good for her teeth, but then I notice that there are two other girls also sucking their thumbs. I haven't seen thumb-sucking since I was a nanny. Seeing a bunch of high school students do it is odd. I need to find out what this means.

"But what's the point?" Vanessa has her skinny, tattooed arms folded across her chest. An intense and sharply carved Latina with flowing black hair that almost reaches her waist, her eyes are lovely but usually narrowed to almost imperceptible brown slits when she is looking at me. "What's the point of writing about our lives or anything else?" She flips her hair over her shoulder and begins to fold it into a loose braid.

"I guess the point is it takes what's here and puts it here," I say, touching my heart and then the blank paper in front of me.

"I don't get it," Vanessa says dismissively. She reaches down to her sock, pulling out a long thread and securing her braid with it.

"You guys carry a lot. Most of you have seen things that kids should never have to see. Even if you had a perfect childhood, you are locked up and that's heavy baggage. Writing allows you to put that down on paper, look at it, hopefully learn from it and then leave it there. The paper is a neutral sounding board. You can tell it all the things you never had the courage to tell a person because they might judge you. The paper can withstand anything you throw at it."

Vanessa's eyes snap at me in double-time, the rose gold cogs slowly beginning to turn. Her lips purse and then relax. "The paper can take it," she says, chin raised. She looks down at the paper in front of her like she is seeing it for the first time. Maybe in a way she is. There came a time in my own life when I saw it for what it really was: a place to unload your cargo, a life raft.

Alexa, a timid and teary-eyed girl with a shaved head, raises her hand for help. "I don't know what to write. I don't have a neighborhood. I consider the world my home."

This is the first time she has spoken aloud in class. All she has done these past two weeks is blink at me like a terrified rabbit, plucking out her eyelashes with trembling fingers. Her voice is startling enough to render me speechless for a moment. It sounds like a little girl's voice, the voice of a kid no more than three or four years old. High-pitched, slightly squeaky, with the soft baby cadence of a child just rising up from her toddler years. The disparity between the voice and the teenage girl it is emitting from is jarring.

"A beautiful idea. Kind of hard to write about the whole world in one hour, though. Perhaps we can narrow it down. Where did you grow up?"

"I grew up in Texas and then downtown San Francisco with my mom."

"Do either of those places feel like home to you?"

"No," she squirms in her seat. "I have been living in group homes for the past four years. Plus me and my mom moved so much, I was never at one place long enough to memorize my address."

I had not expected this. What of the children who have never had a home? How was this writing assignment making them feel? How can I ask a child to write about something they never had?

"So your house never felt like a home to you?"

"No. My mom kept me inside all the time. I was not allowed to ever leave. I couldn't even go to school. I had to clean all day. " She smiles sadly at the horror on my face. "It's okay. It's my past so I am okay with it. I think it scares other people more than it scares me. So that's why I live in the group homes. My mom was a junkie and I was born hooked. I picked it up for real when I was twelve."

"I am sorry. I wish I had better words for you. If there isn't a place that you ever felt was home, then just write about what you want your future home to be like."

"I would live in Portland. I ran away from a group home when I was thirteen and ended up there. It's the perfect city. I would have a little wood house in the forest and I would read Anne Sexton all day and write poetry. I saw that you had Anne Sexton on the bookcase when I came in. That's how I know I can trust you. Anyone who likes Anne Sexton knows pain well."

Wow. Whose little girl is this?

Miranda calls out to me across the room, asking if the foster home she was raised in after her mother went to prison for five years when she was little would count as a home. Miranda is short and stocky, her eyebrows two tattooed brown lines above cat-like hazel eyes. There is a large sore on her upper lip, which she gnaws and picks at throughout the day. The paper she turned in the first day of school didn't have a name on it, but it did have a few drops of blood, so I knew it was hers.

"If it feels like home, then let it be home, I guess."

She begins to write and is only a few sentences in when a guard comes to collect her to take her to court. This is the fifth student that has been pulled out of class just today. Students are constantly being pulled out of class to see mental health, to talk to their probation officer, to go to court, to have their ankle monitors put on, to go to the nurse. It is insanely disruptive and I have a feeling it's not going to get any better. And they are never pulled out at the beginning and returned at the end. They always seem to be taken away as soon as they start something and brought back before the class is officially over so they have no idea what's going on.

"It's really frustrating," I whine at Yvonne after work. We are pulling our purses out of our lockers, both of looking slightly less radiant than when we came in this morning. My hair has gone from nicely tousled to angry seaweed. "I can't make any headway with these kids when they are being pulled out of class every day."

"They are spending a lot more time in class than they normally would on the outs," Yvonne explains. "Most students who are incarcerated have a long history of truancy. Some of these kids started skipping school when they were in third grade."

"How do these kids' parents not notice that their eight year old is not in school? Were they raised by really distracted wolves?"

"A lot of them were raised by single moms or grandmothers or some random family member. Maybe one of the parents is dead. Or in prison. And a third of them are foster kids." Yvonne coils her scarf around her neck. "The parents could both be working two jobs. Or maybe they are illegal immigrants and never enrolled their kid in school."

"Think of each of these kids like a ball. A ball that has been dropped so many times it's no wonder that they got used to always being invisible. They learn to role under the table and just disappear. A child who goes unacknowledged is a child who learns that their actions do not matter. Good or bad, whatever they do is not worthy of recognition. If your parent doesn't notice if you are even in school, then do you think that parent will notice much of anything?" Ralph adds, glancing up from the papers he is grading at the table in the corner of the break room.

This statement saddens and angers me more than I am

prepared for. No more. From now on, none of my students will ever feel invisible in my classroom. I will force myself to trust them and to show them that. I was told to trust none of them, to always suspect, but I can't help but wonder if automatic distrust leads to automatic dishonesty. I will try something different. I will trust all of my students until they give me a reason not to. I am feeling powerful and determined for the first time since I moved up here. I know what I am going to do. I have a plan. *So let them bring on all their problems/ I'll do better than my best.*

There is nothing as wonderful as the sun after eight hours in fluorescent lighting. Wendy, the school psychologist, is unloading a plastic crate of files from her car. At this point, I know her in name only. She is portly and disheveled, her face glistening with sweat. A few plastic barrettes are shoved into her wispy grey hair that whips around in the dry, warm wind. Folders are spilling out of her arms as she attempts to rearrange them while clutching a large mug of coffee. After attempting to assist her and succeeding in only dropping more of the papers onto the ground, I broach the subject that has been bugging me all day: the girl's thumb-sucking.

"It's actually quite common here, especially among the girls. Thumb-sucking is a sort of self-soothing mechanism. It is common among children with a history of severe childhood sexual abuse. Did any of the girls have a voice that sounded like it belonged to a little girl?"

"Yes! Alexa sounded like a ventriloquist dummy being operated by a three year old."

"It's called Little Girl Voice. If a girl is horribly sexually traumatized before the onset of puberty, her voice can just freeze there, usually at the age at which she was molested."

I immediately wished that I had not inquired. Now every time I saw my students sucking their thumbs or heard Alexa speak, I would know that I was looking at the human remnants of childhood sexual abuse, frozen in time.

October 2

"I said open your hand, dammit!"

Carlos throws the chunk of pencil lead into my hand. I had watched him walk to the pencil sharpener, snap the tip with his thumb and attempt to pocket it. Snapping off the tips of pencils is one way that the kids sneak lead back into their cells to either graffiti the walls or carve gang insignias into their skin. Carlos's lanky arms are already covered with puffy scar tissue names and numbers. I give him my best disapproving look and point to the door. Carlos saunters casually to the door where Mr. Robbins is waiting. As they are about to walk away, Mr. Robbins sticks his head back in my classroom and says, "Thank you."

What the hell? That was the first time a guard has thanked me for disciplining a student. It seems an odd remark until I realize that he was thanking me for preventing this student from hurting himself. I am momentarily struck by how much this man must care about these students.

I am really struggling to move forward with the kids, to not settle in this pit of stagnation we are standing in. I had told myself the other day that I would trust them all, completely and fully, but this is proving more difficult than I had anticipated. As much as I want to see them as just kids, life has wizened and hardened them. They can't do geometry but they are masters of angles. I get uncomfortable when one of them walks behind me and then I feel guilty that I am uncomfortable. If any of these kids walked behind me at the library or the grocery store, I wouldn't think twice. But because they are in here, because I know what I know, and because they wear what they wear, Jorge's crossing to the bookcase behind me makes my back stiffen. I want to trust my kids. And I tell them that I do, until they prove that they don't deserve it. I am hoping that if I say this, I will believe it too.

After the success of actually getting them to a write a bit the other day, there has not been much headway. They have dragged their feet through everything, complaining and doing the bare minimum. Schoolwork is just one more thing for them to get through. They are not looking to get anything from it, let alone enjoy it. Maybe that one good day was just a fluke. Maybe this is going to be nothing but an uphill battle that never reaches a peak or plateau. I am Sisyphus in a ponytail and mismatched socks.

"Miss Wehr, would you read my paragraph?" Juan walks up to me at the end of class, his journal thrust open. I am skeptical, unsure if this is some type of test. This kid hasn't asked me for anything since I started here, let alone writing feedback.

I have always hated the color white. White is the color of my dad's shirt when he comes home drunk. White is the color of the apron my mom wears when she cleans white people's houses with white bleach bottles. White is the color of the stuff around my dad's nose when he beats my mom. White is the color of the skin of the men who raid my house in the middle of the night and bring me here. White is everything I hate.

I can't help if wonder if the whiteness of my skin puts me on that list. If it does, he was gracious enough to leave that line out. So I guess that's something. "You did something really difficult here. You put an emotion and an experience with a color. A lot of writers can't do that well, but you made it look easy. That's what talented people do; they make it look easy."

"You know, you don't talk to us like we are locked up. You talk to us like we are regular kids on the outs. Like we are just kids in a class, not criminals. So, I just want to show you appreciation for that." His cheeks flush red with his admission and he tosses the journal onto the table and hurries from the room, having said too much. He has lifted a scale from the armor and showed me a quick glimpse of the heart and the flesh beneath.

This is why I am here. I need to treat my students like they are any other teenagers, enforcing the notion that they are all capable of better. If I cease fighting, so will they. The immensity of this undertaking hits me like a wrecking ball. I am not just their teacher. I am a person who can show them that there are people who will not give up on them, even when they have given up on themselves. I can be encouragement and trust and safety to them, if only for a sliver of their days. Maybe if I believe hard enough that I can reach them, I actually can. *The courage to serve them with reliance/ to face my mistakes without defiance.* Good advice, Julie.

The shadows are already growing long on the drive home, the glass office buildings casting darkness onto the freeway. The graffiti-tagged off-ramp sign indicates right for East Palo Alto. Impulsively, I jerk the steering wheel, careening across three lanes of spotty traffic. The road wraps around to the left and then back over the freeway, past an Ikea and a Nordstrom's Rack, a few other strip-mall essentials. A stoplight is the lone sentinel between this semblance of civilization and what lies beyond it.

Everything shifts dramatically; large empty lots of patchy dead grass and collapsed For Rent signs begin to appear, punctuated by check-cashing places and liquor stores. Mexican markets with today's specials spray-painted on slabs of wood siding and dark-windowed bail bond offices line the main street that runs down the spine of the city.

I pull into the parking lot of a taco joint, a red and beige stucco hacienda with a stenciled sombrero above the door. I shove my notepad and keys into my jacket pocket, jam my purse under the seat and get out of the car. A large man in all black, wearing a stained baseball cap charges across the parking lot at me. His face is sweating despite the chill in the wind, stringy black curls dangling from under his baseball cap.

"Hey you got any change for a burrito?" His brown eyes are milky, a thin line of white spit crusting his lips. "For food, not booze. I just got done working."

I explain I don't have any change, holding up my hands to show that I don't even have a wallet. He turns away wordlessly, shuffling back across the parking lot towards the entrance of the restaurant.

The sidewalk along the main street is thick with cracks, the concrete peaked and valleyed, the old dead roots of trees no longer there breaking up the ground into small, gray hills. There is graffiti everywhere, on lampposts and street signs, on buildings and fences, on piles of abandoned construction refuse. Everyone wants to claim something, to own it.

Residential streets split off from the main drag like limbs on a dying tree. I select one at random and start down it. An old black man on a bicycle pulls up beside me, his gray beard blowing in the breeze. He holds a crushed Coke can in his hand, tapping out a beat on his handlebars to a song that only he can hear. His front tire glides over a red rag on the ground, half draped over a dying cluster of dandelions. He splits silently from me at a church, disappearing around an old willow that stands in the corner of the yard. A homeless man sits on the front steps, smoking a cigarette and staring ahead into nothing.

The street itself is unmarked by a curb of any sort, gradually declining into strips of gravel and dirt which become someone's front yard, littered with crushed Doritos, broken plastic spoons and coat hangers, lone socks, a sparerib crawling with ants. There are no sidewalks. The streets bleed into homes here, no barrier between the two, no safe place.

Every house on this street has a fence around it: chain-link, wood slates, wrought iron. Most are rotting or collapsing in some spots, spotted with 'Beware of Pit Bull' and 'No Trespassing' signs. The chain-link fences sag hopelessly towards the ground, a few with deflated balloons still clinging to them. Two brown pit bull puppies charge a fence, jumping ecstatically and pawing the wood. I reach through and scratch them both. They tumble over one another for my hand, licking and yelping. The wood slates have holes bitten out of the bottom, a few riddled with bullet holes, falling into each other like drunk people. A woman carrying plastic bags of empty cans in both hands limps by, singing in Spanish as she passes a wrought iron fence with a pair of red children's cowboy boots impaled on the spikes.

From the fences, gravel driveways lead up past dirt yards that are somehow barren yet crowded. Craggy mountains of rusted furniture, faded Fisher-Price toys, empty buckets and camper shells with smashed out windows. Mismatched chairs form semi-circles on concrete slabs, split pleather and rickety dining room set rejects. Dogs curl up beneath them, trying to stay warm on the cold ground. There are so many cars in the driveways, each in a state of disrepair. Some are on blocks with an open hood, others covered in weatherworn tarps. The windows of the houses are webbed with cracks, patched with duct tape, and curtained by tin foil and 49er's jerseys. Security bars cover most doors and windows. Beneath the windows, terra cotta pots of cacti and succulents remain stubbornly green, starkly contrasted against the beige and white of the stucco.

Aside from a dog's occasional bark, and the silvery needle of panic from a car alarm, the street is deathly quiet. There are no voices, no trees for the wind to rustle as it passes through, no birds. It is a neighborhood that is holding its breath.

An off-white Cadillac, its bass turned so high that the frame's vibrations overpower the music, slows to a crawl beside me. The inside is too dark to make out anything but a wife beater on the body of a young black man. He speeds up and stops a few yards ahead of me. I keep my head down and quicken my pace. As I pass the car, I can feel his eyes following me. He says nothing, guns the engine again and races a few more yards ahead before stopping again. I shift the pen in my hand so that it could be stabbed into someone's neck and continue walking with my head as low as it can be while still watching where I am going. The car turns around and drives away.

The street dead ends, the cul-de-sac filled with cars. A trash-filled grocery cart with three wheels leans off the side of the road. Two large dogs watch me carefully, one laying on the ground and the other pissing on a tire. From behind one of the cars, a heavily pregnant woman appears. She sees me and stops. We stare at each other for a moment, her wide brown face revealing nothing but suspicion. I stand there awkwardly for a few seconds before I turn around and head back down the way I came. "Hey!" she yells. "You lost, white girl?"

I half turn back towards her, trying to smile and shaking my head. I wave my notepad like it explains something. She stops walking towards me and watches in silence as I walk away.

Back on the main street two guys in a forest green pick-up cat call at a light, hanging out of their windows, "Hey little mama! Whatcha doing tonight?"

It isn't until I am back in my car that I realize I have been holding my breath. A sharp knock at my window makes me jump. On the other side of the glass, another homeless man is standing there, holding a sign for spare change. His wiry white hair has gone yellow at the ends, matching the few teeth left in his tar-rimmed mouth. He shifts his green Army surplus jacket back onto his shoulders and shoves the sign closer to my window, unsure if I am really seeing him.

October 11

The past few weeks of work are finally coming to fruition today. The boys will be typing up the final drafts of their autobiographical narratives that they had been slaving over in class. They have been through one rough draft, two edits, and many hours of writing and erasing. It's been an arduous process, much like trying to convince a bunch of frightened horses to cross a river. It would be so much easier if I could just throw a blanket over their eyes and just make them somehow trust me. And even though the past few weeks of getting them to this point has been some of the hardest work I have ever done, it has brought us a little closer. The boys have moved from resenting and not trusting me to trying to drive me insane.

"Any questions before we head down to the computer lab?"

The boys are eager and grinning, clutching their rough drafts in their hands, occasionally whacking one another with them. The need to make everything into a weapon apparently isn't something that boys ever grow out of.

"Where can I get my hands on a really big bunny?" asks Jesus.

"How does my brain tell my hand to do this?" Carlos rips half a poster off the wall.

"I want to plant a banana tree, but bananas don't have any seeds. How am I supposed to plant a banana tree if they don't have any seeds?" demands Antonio.

"I meant questions about what you are going to do with your essay. My fault. I should have been more specific."

There was a palpable excitement as the group sauntered into the computer lab. In the hallway, they laugh loudly and wave at acquaintances in the other classes we pass by. At the computers, they rapidly click the mouses and pound at the keyboards for a few seconds before realizing they needed to turn the monitors on.

The first twenty minutes go smoothly enough. They type, occasionally asking spelling and grammar related questions. My seams are splitting with the pride I am trying to contain, fighting the urge to hug every one of the boys and tell them how amazing they are.

Jorge raises his hand and announces that he is done and ready to print. He walks to the solitary printer on the old desk at the head of the classroom. And he waits. And waits.

"Try clicking print again, Jorge."

He returns to his computer, clicks it a few times. "Now the goddamn screen is frozen! Man, fuck this shit!" Jorge throws his rough draft against the wall. The papers shatter against the concrete blocks, a rage of white spraying out across the room.

In three more minutes, three more computers froze up. The printer is still not working. Mr. Robbins is elbow deep in the working of it when he straightens up and sighs, "No luck."

"Maybe we can save them. I can print them out at a later time." This is how a drowning victim feels.

"I ain't saving shit. I don't want no one seeing this. You promised that only you would see it. If it's on here, anyone can get at it," Jorge growls. "I put my personal history into this, my family and my childhood. You said no one else would see this. You broke your promise!"

"How about a disk? Would you mind if I saved it on a disk?"

He shrugs and stares at the wall, frozen as these fucking computers. Across the room Carlos and Jesus get up and walk to the door, pretending to grab Kleenex on the way so they have an excuse to stick their heads out of the room and assess the hallway to see where the next closest guard was.

"You two! Sit down!" I bark at them. "Mr. Robbins, where are the disks?"

"There are none. Where do you think you are? A school?" He meant this jokingly but he can see how squarely this hits me in his chest. "I can check if someone has a flash drive."

I try to smile, forcing my gratitude at his presence to overpower my unease at the complete disintegration of my carefully structured lesson. By now all the boys are done but unable to go onto the printing step in the assignment, leaving a frustrated cluster in the corner of the room. They speak low to each other in frantic Spanish, eyes darting around the room. There are no books or games in the computer lab so I have nothing to distract them with.

But their eyes, their eyes just destroyed me. They were disappointed, but not at all surprised at being so. I had done exactly what they had expected me to; I had let them down.

"No zip drive," Mr. Robbins announces, striding back into the room.

"This is how it always is." Juan shakes his head. "They say they want us to do good and shit. Be successful and everything. But they won't pay for us to have anything that actually works. How the hell are we supposed to do good when everything here is broken?"

The honesty and the despair in this statement breaks me in half. This young man is absolutely correct. How can they excel when we are not giving them the proper tools? Why the hell is nothing working? How dare my students be given anything but the best. They are used to a life of second bests, hand-me-downs, living below the poverty line, not having the same opportunities as the more financially fortunate. This school is an opportunity for them to overcome those obstacles. Yet the hard work that I have dragged out of them over these past few weeks has been dashed because of out-of-date, malfunctioning equipment that the county has yet to fix due to budgetary issues. All of my students went out on a limb for me. They trusted me enough to actually work for me. They worked hard, producing beautiful, powerful essays about their pasts and they have nothing to show for their work. My greatest fear is that they will give up because of this. Instead of being a catalyst for change and improvement, I will have actually been the one who made them give up entirely. I will have destroyed something that I was supposed to protect.

During lunch I pace the break-room, ranting about school funding and shoddy equipment, throwing a rubber band ball back and forth between my trembling hands. The rest of the teachers eat their sandwiches and salads, watching me amusedly. Am I taking this too seriously? Too personally? I can't help it. I could feel my kid's disappointment. Watching them trudge out of the room without their final papers in their hands was an absolutely sad moment.

A technician is called in after lunch from the county office to Band-Aid the computers until a more long-term plan can be figured out and funded. Portly and gray-ponytailed, he rubs his three-day stubble and pushes his glasses back up his nose.

"Please tell me you can save their work from the computers. Otherwise one of us is going out the window."

"You remember that scene from the first Teenage Mutant Ninja Turtles movie where Raphael comes back from a fight and yells about losing a sai? You remember what Splinter says?"

"Then it is lost."

"Yep. Figured it would soften the blow if I worked the Ninja Turtles into it."

As my Sureno class straggles in, I notice some pencil markings on one of the keyboards: *Sur 5103* followed by three dots in a triangular formation. Sureno tagging. This doesn't make sense. The only class in here today was the Norteno class. The Surenos haven't been given pencils yet.

Mr. Robbins is escorting the Nortenos to science class when I pull him aside and explain what had happened. "There is Sureno tagging on a keyboard."

"Well, that is your Sureno class."

"But they don't have any pencils yet. The only group that had pencils in here was the Nortenos. It doesn't make any sense. Why would a Northern tag Southern stuff?"

"Sometimes they will try to get the Surenos in trouble by tagging like them in really obvious places. They think they are pretty clever. Who sat there? I'll go grab him."

Mr. Robbins leaves the room and moments later returns with a distraught and agitated Carlos. His eyes are flashing daggers as I meet him at the doorway. He scans the room full of his enemies with disgust. They are all returning his hate, ounce for ounce.

"I didn't do nothing!" Carlos yells into my face before I even get a chance to say anything.

"You were the one sitting at that desk."

"I didn't do it! Why the fuck would I tag scrap shit?"

Mr. Robbins is standing beside him impassively, with a look that says there is nothing you can say that I haven't heard. The Surenos stiffen noticeably at the word scrap. A few shoot each other glances. A chair screeches sharply as one of them pivots, turning his frame towards Carlos and leaning forward with his hands clasped together.

"What the hell does that word mean?" I keep hearing that word in my Norteno's conversations and I know it must be bad because they always seem to spit it out like a sour strawberry.

"Scrap is what our Norteno boys here call the Surenos. It's gang slang. If you hear any of these knuckleheads say that, you need to kick them out of class," Mr. Robbins explains.

"So that's what it means." I need to do like 300 retroactive time-outs.

"Can I go back now?" Carlos is whining.

"Yea, you can go back. Back to your room." Mr. Robbins pulls the radio off his hip and lets the cellblock know one of the kids is coming back.

"But it wasn't me." His voice is arcing into a whine.

And frankly, I don't know if it was. I didn't see him do anything and I am not in the habit of punishing a student for something that I am not sure that they did. But the institution has rules and this is one of them. Part of me is cracking, too. Am I sending an innocent boy back to his cell? The problem is I am not very experienced at dealing with people who have made a living out of lying. I always thought honesty was the default option and kids lied when cornered, but these children have learned that all tracks must be covered, which leads them to lie at all times, just to stay in form. I watch Mr. Robbins lead Carlos away, knowing that having him in class again tomorrow will be a whole other world of hell to deal with.

That night I sit on my front steps with a glass of red wine, reflecting back on the disaster of the day. It's not just the shortcomings that bother me. I don't feel like I am doing enough. Teaching kids how to write essays and understand grammar is important, of course. But how is it actually shaping and changing lives? I don't just want to be a good teacher. I want to be an amazing teacher. That *Dangerous Minds/ Freedom Writers/ Stand and Deliver* earthshaking, life-changing educator. The teacher whose classes are punctuated by milestones and revelations, all backed up with a tender soundtrack.

The problem with those movies is that all of the drivel is cut out. The days of grammar drills that even the most creative teacher struggles to make engaging and the most enthusiastic of students struggle to feign interest in. Those movies don't show the copious amounts of paperwork that come with teaching. Besides lesson planning, grading, and state-wide test preparation and administration, there is a constant stream of paperwork to be filled and filed with Human Resources, substitute plans to maintain, IEPs to attend, ongoing training, periodic observations, curriculum seminars, not to mention that a teacher is never just a teacher. From coaching after school sports to assisting in extracurricular activities, to working on curriculum development and engaging in administrative tasks, a teacher has to be part secretary, part administrator, part therapist, part mentor, along with a plethora of other roles. On a limited budget. With significant and ever-increasing restraints and constrictions from district and state levels. Being a teacher, a good teacher, is not an easy job. I laugh at those who have the ignorance and gall to comment on how nice it must be to get off work at three. You don't get off at three. You keep working after three, you just don't get paid for it.

October 12

Asshole is the first word that comes to mind. Yesterday, I was right about today being a challenging one. I had just assumed the difficulties would be as a result of students, not the staff.

One of the more helpful and frustrating aspects of working at juvenile hall is the presence of the guards, also known as group supervisors and commonly referred to as staff. Their job is to maintain peace among the inmates and ensure security for students and staff alike. While the school side of the property is technically our domain, we are constantly reminded through both word and action, that this is probation department territory.

I have not had any real issues with the staff. They have always been helpful, if a bit removed. The two staff that are in my classroom the most, Mr. Thompson and Mr. Robbins, have been helpful and kind.

It's easy to see someone as their job, especially when that's all you know of them. Aside from a last name and a general physical description that could be helpful to a really talented forensic artist, I know nothing about the people who stand between bodily harm and me. They have histories, families, interests, quirks and identities, all of which are unknown to me. They are a name in a county-issued sweatshirt much like my students, separated by a paycheck and a pair of handcuffs. It's odd to work with someone for over a month and know nothing about them. Not that there is ever any time to actually get to know them. What little time we spend in the same space, I spend teaching and they spend watching. Our interactions are limited to the perfunctory greetings and inane small talk. So maybe mild pleasantry is all I can realistically expect. They aren't even obligated to be polite, so I should really be grateful that they have all been. There is, however, one notable exception.

It was a cold Wednesday and I had gone to one of the units to drop off some paperwork for Juan. After devouring every Anthony Bourdain book in the classroom collection, Juan had decided to put his voracious appetite and love of strenuous work to good use and pursue a career as a chef. The kids here are not allowed internet access so I had printed out some information for him on enrolling in culinary school. Juan was excited to have a vocational opportunity where his strikes wouldn't automatically disqualify him.

A tall African-American man stood at the edge of the guard's station, rifling through a green folder, his high forehead creased in consternation. The boys were in the middle of lunchtime, scattered around the unit at the metal tables and digging into plastic trays of iceberg lettuce salads and nachos. I approached the man, proffering the folder and asking if he could give it to Juan once he was finished with his meal. Stepping out from behind the corner of the station, I saw the sweatshirt he wore indeed bore the name of the county but his white Velcro-strapped shoes gave it away. He was an inmate.

"Well you just lost all credibility." The voice came from above.

Looking up, I saw a guard standing above me in the elevated box that is the station. He was tall and thick, black hair buzzed short. The lines across his pale, shiny brow were deep enough to tuck rice into, with even deeper ones running parallel to his thin lips. He looked like a hostile Charlie McCarthy. There was a harshness in his eyes that said that he had been doing this kind of work for way too long and was more interested in quiet than rehabilitation. I blinked stupidly, waiting for him to say that he was joking. It didn't come. He continued to glare down at me, thick arms folded across his massive ribcage.

"I am the new English teacher." Maybe he had no idea who I was. Maybe he thought I was some idiot white girl who had wandered into juvenile hall by mistake. Maybe he was from a country where people were in a constant competition to see who could be the rudest.

"I know who you are." He turned his back to me and walked away.

"You caught Mr. Walsh on a good day," Mr. Robbins chuckled from his perch on the counter of the station. "Lucky you."

Mr. Walsh has been on my case since then. Whenever he is patrolling the hall of the school, he hovers in front of my open classroom door. Annoyingly, doors must be kept open at all times to allow the guards to pick up on the first signs of a fight. While this is supposed to be a security measure, it actually hampers classroom productivity since students get distracted by everyone who walks by and the guards radios and incessant chatter to one another is very loud and disruptive. Maybe my mistaking a tall white guy in a dark sweatshirt who is an inmate for every other tall white guy in a dark sweatshirt who actually works there has shoved me into a suspicious light. I am now just one more person he has to watch.

Today Mr. Walsh is lurking in my doorway, his glares at me interrupted periodically by his snarls at the boys. They are having a lively discussion, if a bit raucous. Mr. Walsh shakes his head sporadically, rolling his eyes whenever I look at him.

It's a blatant fallacy that a classroom has to be quiet. The idea that children learn best when being totally silent is such an asinine one that I wonder what irritated, control freak teacher ever decided that it should be quid pro quo for their classroom. Discussion is one of the best ways for kids to learn, especially my kids. Discussion shows that they have ideas, good ones, and they are worth sharing. Maybe they have been talked to too much and it's time for them to just be listened to. And getting a lively discussion going was one of the hardest things I have done in the class yet. So many topics just slipped through their fingers: presidential choices (they were either minors or felons and could not vote), the Iraqi war (they had their own war to fight), dream vacations (every one of them was living below poverty level). So when I found a foothold in the topic of prejudice and social discrimination, I sat back and let them talk. Their thoughts and experiences pour out of them in churning waves, every one of them having been touched in some way by people whose minds only form of exercise was jumping to conclusions. I ask the boys if they can think of anyone whose prejudice made them notorious.

"Like Biggie Smalls?" asks Jorge.

"Hitler!" calls out Kevin.

"Excellent! What was he known for?"

"Killing the Jews, only liking white people, and starting World War II," Juan adds. He thinks for a moment. "And inventing Haagen Dazs ice cream."

"Wow. I did not know that Hitler invented ice cream. He

really was misjudged, wasn't he?" Smiling, I glance over at Mr. Walsh to see if he has caught the humor in this as well. His face is unchanging as a gargoyle. And about as pleasant looking.

"If Hitler was around today, would he be in jail?" asks Marco. "I know he would be hella old and shit."

"You can be old and still be a bad ass," says Carlos.

"But would he still be a threat?"

"I don't think old criminals are a real big issue. All old people wanna do is hang out and like...I don't know...eat soup," Kevin says. He glances up at me, checking that I have noticed his contribution to the dialogue.

I am especially proud of Kevin's progress over the past month. His long hair that usually falls into his eyes and provides a barrier between him and everyone else is pulled out of his face, revealing his bright brown eyes and a very nice smile. He is genuinely trying and I am trying to encourage him as much as I can, but every time I think I am gaining ground with him, he retreats. And when I give him the space I think he wants, he clamors for my attention. It's been a push me, pull you sort of engagement. It reminds me of a toddler I used to babysit who would cry to be picked up, and when you did, he would fight to get back down onto the floor. Sometimes I feel like I am trying to grab the hand of a drowning victim who thinks I am the one who pushed him into the water in the first place.

"You guys are being too loud!" From the doorway, Mr. Walsh is yelling into my classroom. Every head in the classroom spins towards him, including mine. His eyebrows arch in challenge. I decide to cross the room and speak to him face to face instead of yelling back my response across the room and disrespecting him the way he just did to me.

"Because they are sharing their opinions? They are using words instead of knives. This is a classroom. They can have discussions." My lips are shaking with anger and fear. This is the first adult I have had to stand up to in years and it's making me feel ten years old again. I can feel the boys eyes burrowing into the back of my head. They are studying me to see how I deal with confrontation and disrespect. It's only the onus of setting a good example that is keeping me from launching into a barrage of expletives. This man has just challenged my authority in front of my students, in my classroom. If I came into the unit and did the same thing to him, he would be writing a grievance on me so fast, it would make my head spin. Yet I am supposed to back down just because he has a walkie-talkie?

Mr. Walsh looks calmly over my shoulder and calls out, "Kevin! Let's go!"

"What? Why?" Kevin is confused, and looks to me for help. Why is he doing this? Kevin's eyes plead with me and I realize I am totally powerless to save him from a bully with a radio on his belt.

"Get your ass up, Kevin. You can't learn to shut your mouth." Mr. Walsh's gargoyle grimace has morphed into a Grinch grin. This isn't about Kevin at all; it's about me. Mr. Walsh is asserting his dominance over his dominion. A dog pissing on a hydrant is subtler.

Kevin gets up, his shoulders hunched over, his eyes thrown to the floor. The few sparks of passion that had glittered so brightly a few moments ago have been squelched, ground out like a cigarette ember. His hair has begun to fall back into his face.

October 21

The boys file in, their arms tucked behind them, mischief spread across their faces. Jose, Juan, and Antonio stop at my desk, grinning like little kids who just got away with something.

"What are you guys up to?" I smile, standing as they circle my desk. A smarter teacher would be concerned. Thankfully, I am not that smart.

From behind their backs come origami hearts, each hand clutching a paper testament to their acceptance. I am speechless. I will myself not to burst into tears. This is the sort of sweetness that has no place in these concrete walls. "Wow, guys. Thank you." My heart is no longer my own.

Antonio shifts from one foot to another, mumbling, "We wanted to get you something nice, but being in here it's hard."

"I could not have asked for anything better. Diamonds can only aspire to this level of beauty."

"I always get my women nice things." His demeanor shifts from bashful to bold, his neck straightening slightly.

"Well, considering that I am not your woman, this is just the right gift. Thank you."

Antonio narrows his eyes as he stares at my neck. I feel a hot flash of warning until I remember that I am wearing a gold locket around my neck. What idiot wears jewelry into juvenile hall?

"Like that necklace. That's a nice necklace." His eyes narrow, analyzing. The same kid that stood before me a moment ago is no longer here. My necklace has triggered something hungry and eager in him.

"Thank you." I say, instinctively covering it with my hand.

"Can I see it?" He takes a step towards me. There is no malice or threat, just the dark edge of curiosity.

"You can see it from there."

"No, I mean SEE IT. With my hand. For a little while."

"So you want to steal it."

"Well when you say it like that, it just sounds bad." The hardness of him has receded, humor eclipsing warning like a swollen moon.

Charming. Maybe his grandfather was a snake. I distribute a

half-finished idiom sheet and explain to the kids that their job is to finish the idioms and if they don't know one, to just fill in what they think would make sense. I brace myself for the protesting and am shocked when there is none. I stand before them, speechless for a good minute or so before I remember to sit down. Something has shifted here and I don't know what to do with this newness. They are working independently and for a few minutes, they do not need me. They are charging into deeper water and I have to wait for their help signal.

"Alright, let's share out. Jorge, blood is thicker than..."

"Random people."

"Jose, you can't beat a dead..."

"Fish."

Antonio turns around and stares at Jose. "Fish? Where the hell you get fish from?"

"I dunno. It just made sense. Fuck on up out of my fish, homie."

"Antonio, what did you get for 'don't cry over...'?"

"I got don't cry over girls," he reads from his paper.

"That's good advice right there," Jesus nods, pointing at Antonio.

"Jesus? You have one to share with us?"

"Don't put all your eggs on your head," he looks smugly around the room.

"Don't put all your eggs on your head? The hell kind of advice is that?" Juan asks.

"It's damn good advice. You ever see people walking around with eggs on their head? No, cause it would be stupid."

"Well, you can't argue with logic. How about lights are on but...?"

"Lights are on but clothes are off," Marco smiles slyly. This kid walks a constant line, his charm saving him from plunging off either side.

"The pot calling the kettle...?"

"Corn!" Jesus yells out. "That right? No? Kettle corn! You never heard of kettle corn? Come on! That's some good shit right there!"

"It's very tasty. But it's the pot calling the kettle black, not corn."

"I like kettle corn better," he grumbles, crossing his arms.

Eduardo is staring silently at his paper, with that I- wish-I-was-invisible look on his face. Being the mean teacher that I am, I call on him.

"Rome was not built for you," he says through clenched teeth.

I call on Juan for the last idiom on the sheet. "A bird in the hand..."

"Will bite your fucking hand."

October 29

Thursday broke open like an egg. I teetered into it on three hours of sleep and the beginnings of a flu. Flushed and borderline feverish, I am not looking forward to dealing with the terrible triplets. A day in the hall drinks all of your resources and when they are already depleted, you end up in a deficit by three o'clock.

My unholy trio swagger in, chests puffed up and fists clenched. They spread across the room like a fish net. Their energy is intense, bordering on overwhelming. Everyday I brace myself for these three kids, repeating in my head that these are just students. I love all of my students; I just don't like them very much sometimes.

Jesus, Carlos, and Jorge have proven themselves to be particularly difficult. As I have gotten to know them over the past two months, I have seen new parts of them and found out more about them which makes it difficult for me to look at them with anything other than frustration, irritation, and bit of fear. Jesus is the tallest of the group and at seventeen, has three kids from three different women. He is loud, inconsiderate, and boisterous. Jorge fluctuates between sullen and hostile. He is the angriest boy I have ever met, the human version of a boiling pot. You try to reach out and get burned. Carlos is as sleazy as they get, a deadbeat father of twin baby girls that he has never met, and a rap sheet as long as his arm. He has been coming to the hall since he was twelve. He is the one that must always be watched. A thief through and through, he is constantly trying to steal things from every classroom.

At least one of them is kicked out of a class every day and they are all long term inmates, each serving at least nine months. These are boys who are not through with their destructive lifestyle. They are still proudly claiming their neighborhood, remorseless about their actions (it was all the cop's fault or the judge was racist), and basically treat everything that has happened to them as a joke. These are boys who have been cycling through the system for years and will continue until something enormous and unprecedented happens.

What I can't understand is how any lifestyle that involves friends dying and spending time in jail would hold any sort of appeal to anyone with rational thought capacity. My students are very, very smart. These boys could survive anywhere. Their knowledge is one of survival, the ability to rapidly analyze situations and read people, how to seek confrontation and avoid it when necessary.

Jesus comes in, popping off a few rounds from an imaginary gun. I shake my head at him, slightly unnerved at a teenager who misses weapons so much that he turns his hands into guns.

"What? I didn't do nothing." He hikes up his pants, and swaggers to his seat.

Eduardo, who is only fifteen years old and has been in Juvenile Hall twelve times already, comes in next. Today he takes a seat by the wall, near the front of the room. He requires preferential seating since he is legally blind (his mom cannot afford glasses and it takes about five months for a kid to get some in here), and he has a very hard time focusing on what the teacher is saying. Eduardo hears voices but has never been in school long enough to complete psychiatric testing, so I often have to repeat myself over and over to him because he is never sure if I am telling him to do something or if it's one of the voices in his head. I ask him if he plans on reserving a room here for the next three years as I hand him his folder. He shrugs and mutters that he is going to try not to.

"Do or do not do. There is no try," I say in my best Yoda voice. The reference slips past him like an eel.

"I mean, I am going to try. But I will probably be back." He always gives the bare minimum, both academically and conversationally. It is such hard work getting to him. He notices that I am still standing beside him and glancing up, mutters, "Please don't take it personal, Miss Wehr."

How is anything worth this? I understand the need to belong to something, to feel respected and supported, but when the price is your freedom, is it really worth it? And I can't help but make it personal. What am I not doing to make this kid see this for what it really is? I cannot reach Eduardo. Talking to him is like skidding down the cold, slick front of a glacier. The angry boys, like Jorge, may have out of control emotions but at least they haven't had all the human parts of them ripped out by trauma and psychosis. Out of control anger may scare me, but at least I can understand it. Emotions, no matter how frightening, are at least a foothold in understanding another person. But this withdrawal, this complete shutting down and turning inward; there is nothing for me to grab and it makes me feel helpless. There is no handle in him that I can hold onto.

Carlos is in a mood today. He marches to his seat in the farthest corner from the board, throwing himself into it with a disgusted sigh. Carlos will not be allowed to poison this class. If he makes one wrong step, I will kick him out. He will not distract the other students, who are noticeably put off by the hostility radiating out of him, all of them casting furtive glances towards him. I have to lay the line for him and protect the integrity of the classroom somehow, even if it means pushing a component out of it.

I am lecturing on the structure of the research paper when Carlos turns to Jesus and begins to talk to him, casually but loudly enough to let me know that he will do whatever the hell he wants. I recognize this move. I spent half of my high school career in dominance battles with my poor teachers.

"Carlos, this is your only warning," I tell him sharply.

He glares at me, but shuts his mouth. A minute or two passes as I continue the lecture. Then he begins to sing, staring at me, defiant and daring me to stop him.

"That's it!" I am pissed. I start toward the door to summon Mr. Thompson who has rolled his chair out of my sight-line.

"What? I didn't do nothing! HEY! I DIDN'T DO NOTHING!" Carlos is out of his seat, charging towards me. His fists are balled at his sides and his stride is hell-bent and hurried. I stick my hand out the door, frantically signaling the guards who are halfway down the hallway.

"FUCKING BITCH TEACHER!" Carlos is charging across the room towards me, throwing desks out of his way.

Mr. Thompson and Mr. Robbins break into a run. They storm into the room just as Carlos flips the table in front of me, sending books and papers flying across the classroom. I close my eyes and tuck my arms up into my chest, covering my lungs like that's what Carlos is after. Always the best thing to do when confronted with violence. The guards grab him by the shoulders and drag him out, Carlos struggling and demanding that they stop touching them.

I am shaken. I hope not visibly so. The rest of the students have stayed seated and silent, knowing that one wrong move in that type of situation gets them in trouble, too. My mind is hot and frantic. I kneel down to collect the scattered papers. Juan and Jose rise from their seats silently, help me collect the items that have made it all the way across the room. I keep my face blank, somehow willing myself not to cry. They scoop the papers into misshapen piles, refusing to look me in the face. Perhaps looking into a frightened face is just too much. All I know is that I can't show that this has impacted me at all. To show fear means that some of the students may utilize this weakness to their advantage later. Yvonne told me how she made the mistake of showing fear after a string of eight fights occurred in her classroom during one summer, several resulting in school being cancelled while blood was being mopped up. Once the students knew that she had been scared by these instances they played on that anxiety, making loud noises and dropping things in class just to watch her jump.

Yet, I am not sensing any of this in the boys. They are quiet but seem worried, watching me intently. Eduardo's face is almost registering something that could pass as sympathy.

"There you go, Miss Wehr," murmurs Jose, handing me the folders he collected. "Sorry about that. He gets that way sometimes. It's not you."

Trying to organize the pile of one hundred notebooks into the separate classes that they were split into is futile, my hands feel numb and useless. I set the pile down and grin to myself a bit. This was the first time I have been called a fucking bitch by someone I was not dating.

There is no mention for the rest of class as to what just happened, no acknowledgment of the violence or abnormality. Their ability to transition from something as unsettling as this to working calmly at their desks unsettles me more than Carlos's outburst. What on earth could have possibly happened to my kids to have prepared them for this?

November 9

If there is one thing that is consistent in a juvenile facility, it's inconsistency. Between the roster of students that changes at least once a day to the continual undercurrent of insecurity regarding the stability of our jobs in a place where the population fluctuates every month and is currently at an all-time low, every day is spent between land-minds and eggshells. In a comprehensive high school, students are given projects that take various amounts of time to complete. English staples such as writing essays and reading novels all take weeks to complete and in a court school, they are almost impossible.

You may start a project on Monday with seventeen students in one class. On Tuesday one of the kids leaves and two new kids come to class. On Wednesday you are teaching on the units because of fog, so your students that are normally in one class are spread throughout four different cell blocks. So you have to teach something else because each class is at a different point in whatever book you are reading. Thursday you are back in the class, but one kid is in court, another kid got released, and a third is serving a 24 hour in cell detention. So when they come back tomorrow, they will be way behind. On Friday, you get two more new kids who have missed all the work leading up to today. Another kid is pulled out to talk to his lawyer and halfway through class, the school is shut down because of a fight in another classroom.

Over-arching lesson plans are inadvisable at best. My well-meaning colleagues had cautioned me against reading novels or plays in class, as kids will constantly be coming in halfway through with no idea what the hell is going on. But the more I am advised against something, the more intriguing it becomes.

The Lion in Winter seems a great place to start. Witty, acerbic, and scandalous, it is the perfect introduction to plays. It's also my favorite and I really struggle to teach anything that I don't love. It goes back to being a terrible liar. I have no poker face and my emotions always read like a giant neon sign in my eyes. But I can sell anything I believe in.

The problem is this play has a lot of antiquated vocabulary in it, a lot of weird words that most people don't use in their day-to-day conversations. I can't remember the last time I used the phrase 'tinker's dam'. And this may be too difficult of a play to start the boys off with. They may try to rise to it, become discouraged and recede like the tide. But I have to try, the driving force behind those who are relentlessly hopeful.

"Miss Wehr!" Jose is already whining at the vocabulary sheet I have placed on his desk. He drags his hands dramatically through his thick black hair until he realizes that he is messing up the perfectly gelled coiffure he spent a great deal of time on. He hurriedly pats his hair back into place. "I don't need to learn any vocabulary. I know all these words already." He has been drawing lines in the sand for days.

"I will make you a deal. I will ask you what a few of them mean. If you know them, you don't have to do this assignment. First word: widowhood."

"It's the place where the wives of the dead homies hang out."

"Wrong. Next: flourish."

He scrunches up his lips into a pucker, his eyes frantically searching the walls for help or clues. "To polish the floor."

"Wrong. Last one, cobbler."

"It's that freaky looking rat dog that nobody can find. You know...the Chaupacobbler."

"Do the assignment, Jose."

"Hella shady," he sighs, scrawling his name on the paper.

The amount of slang that my students weave into their sentences is nothing short of depressing. Every day there seems to be a new word that they use which I need translated. I try to explain to them that slang has no place in higher education or work environments. All I get are a dozen pairs of blinking eyes. They are hearing but not listening. I know that look very well. I spent years of my life giving it to well-meaning teachers.

When I try to tell them the more socially acceptable equivalent of what they have just said, they accuse me of trying to make them talk like white people which ultimately leads into a discussion of how one presents oneself verbally greatly impacts how others view us and how sounding ignorant is almost worse than actually being ignorant. Every question or statement or discussion branches out into dozens more. These kids are so hungry to know things, so full of questions, so eager to understand their world. I tell them this is why they must go to college, or at the very least surround themselves with intelligent, curious people and read everything they possibly can. My hope is that one day they won't have to ask questions like 'can you survive with only one kneecap?' and 'is a sheep the same thing as a female goat?'

Perhaps even more imperative than their language deficits is the need to address and abolish the raging sexism and homophobia that has become commonplace among these young men. The boys, clinging to the machismo that drives the majority of their thoughts and actions, find the idea of homosexuality so repulsive that they treat it as a perverse joke. This may have subconsciously factored into my choosing *The Lion in Winter*. One of the central characters, Prince Richard, defies every gay stereotype. He is a vicious and violent hyper- masculine solider. I am hoping that being introduced to a non-stereotypical gay character will change their attitudes towards homosexuality. Or at the very least, help them to realize that they don't know everything yet.

Someone once said that attitude is simply a habit of the mind. To change an attitude, you need to start changing the habits that your mind accepts as truth. It is presumptive of me to assume that I can change my student's attitudes or even their habits. But I can expose them to things that make the unfamiliar not so foreign and the inaccessible, accessible. Enter literature, stage left.

Before we begin *The Lion in Winter*, I take a class period to discuss twelfth century England. The story line is convoluted and it requires a fair amount of background knowledge about not only the history, but also an explanation of each character, as they are fairly complex.

I hand out Post-Its for the boys to write down questions they have about the lecture, but by the time I have finished distributing them, they have become an assortment of brightly colored monocles, Hitler mustaches, and one pair of lopsided booby tassels.

"Did I say write a question on your Post-It or turn it into an eye patch, Juan?"

"The first one. But you were thinking the second one,"

Juan says, his pink Post-It clinging to his eyebrow.

I launch into a brief background of the Plantagenets and the kids seem surprisingly engaged. A few are even writing down questions. Feeling braver, I begin to explain that Prince Richard is keeping a secret from his family.

"He's gay," Jorge guesses, chuckling to himself.

This is common among the boys. They find homosexuality to be funny, a sort of perverse joke that is so ridiculous, it's amusing. With all the women in the world, why would a man choose to be with another man? The faces of the boys crunch into themselves like empty soda cans when my silence affirms this.

"Wait, hold up. So this guy in the play is a faggot?" Jesus holds his hand up like a stop sign as he speaks.

I have to remind myself that boundaries and knowing what is and is not appropriate is not a strong point among these students. It is my job to gently redirect them towards a more socially acceptable discourse. "That term has no place in this classroom. It's derogatory. Watch your language."

"That homosexual. That guy fucks other guys?"

"Find another word." Half of my day is spent trying to get my students to adopt less offensive synonyms.

"That guy does other guys?"

"He is a gay man. But there is no sex in the play, if that's what you are concerned about." I suddenly find myself deeply exhausted and sink into an empty desk, every part of me heavy and aching. I don't think I have the strength to climb this mountain with them.

Jesus nods slowly as the rest of the boys watch him, gauging his reaction. Surprisingly, he does not completely shut himself out of the lesson. The rest of the character explanations go smoothly, until it comes time to divvy up the roles. Hands shoot up for King Henry and the two straight princes. The boys even volunteer to read for the Queen Eleanor and Princess Alais, but no one raises their hands to read for Prince Richard.

"It's just a part in a play," I reiterate, but they are not budging. Offering to read the words of a gay man would throw their own sexuality into a suspicious light in the eyes of their peers. This is riskier than anything they have done in the streets. "Oh, for

God's sake. I will read it." My frustration and resignation has swallowed any excitement I had ten minutes ago about starting this play with them.

"Wait, no. You are a woman. You should read a woman's part. You can't read a gay guy's part." Antonio looks more confused and slightly alarmed than angry.

"I don't have an issue with gay people. And reading the part in a play of a gay man no more makes me a homosexual than wearing a leather belt makes me a cow."

"Being gay ain't right," grumbles Jorge.

"Says who?" This is just pure irritation talking at this point, never a good mouth to speak out of.

"Jesus." Jorge glares at me, daring me to disagree.

"What?" Jesus looks up from his desk.

"No, man. Jesus. God's little homie."

"So you think that being gay is wrong because Jesus said so? How do we even know that's what he believed?"

"Cause that's what it says in the Bible."

"Who wrote the Bible?" I feel the ghost of every Christian high school teacher standing above me and glaring. It's a fine line to walk, trying to get someone to look at their own beliefs without seeming critical of them.

"Jesus?" Jose suggests, that look of concern that he gets when he is afraid he is going to have to realize a truth he doesn't want to eclipsing his face.

"What?" Jesus was getting frustrated.

"Not you, homie! Pay attention!"

"The bible was written by men. Regular old humans," I explain.

"Oh. Well, it was written by guys that heard Jesus say those things. Eye witnesses." Marco chimes in.

"Can eye witnesses ever be wrong? We are only people. We can make mistakes. How many times have you and a friend done something and then retold the story later and your versions were not identical?"

"So you saying it ain't true?" Jesus rubs the rosary beads tattooed on his wrist. They wrap around the four dots he received when he was jumped into his gang, a marriage of belief and obligation.

"Not at all. It could be. Anything can be. It could have all happened just the way it was written. Or it could be a bunch of stories that got passed from person to person and perhaps got changed as they did."

"I live by the Bible," Jorge sneers. "Nothing you can say will change that."

"What part of the Bible advocates armed robbery?"

"Well, I live by parts of the Bible." Jorge flushes and clears his throat.

"But it's okay to believe in religion, isn't it?" Juan's eyes are desperate and pleading for an affirmation I do not have to give.

"Of course it is! You can believe in anything you want!" My voice shakes with the heaviness of this.

November 15

Perhaps the most disturbing are the broken children, the children who were robbed of their innocence through molestation and sexual abuse. A lot of these kids are so emotionally disturbed and damaged that they are not allowed to mix with the regular population and are kept on a separate unit called the SMU or Special Management Unit. SMU also houses kids that are trying to leave their gangs and risk being attacked if they are around other boys and most of the boys who have been charged with sexually related crimes. Sex offenders are known as blue-dotters because of the blue sticker on their files. Occasionally these children come to school but having been qualified for special education services due to their emotional disturbances, attend a separate class down the hallway. There are also students who have not yet gone through the long and arduous qualifying process for special education and attend the mainstream classes, even though their behavior and academic performance is clearly a cry for help. This is equally difficult for them and for the teachers as the students are not mentally capable of dealing with the rigor and rules of a 'regular' classroom and can range from being non-productive and hostile to outright confrontational and sexually inappropriate.

On Monday I had my first encounter with this population. Walking into work, Yvonne says that there was a fight the night before on one of the units and as a result the kids were on lock down, meaning that all of the teachers had to go teach on the cellblocks. School starts in half an hour. My lesson plan for today requires the use of a white board and the projector, neither one of which is available on the cellblock. The hardest part of this is that the students were no longer broken up into their school groups. Rather, each class would be made up of every student on the unit. No more separating the kids by their gang affiliation. They would all be mushed together.

Realizing that all their folders were broken up by the school groupings, not the housing groupings, I pull them all out of their respective shelves and began to rifle through them. All the blue kids go in one pile, all the greens in another, and so forth until I have five color-coordinated stacks. By the time I have split the folders, sharpened the pencils, and photocopied enough worksheets to keep the kids occupied for an hour, I am five minutes late for first period. I charge up the pathway to the one of the housing units, predictably the one farthest away from the school. The guards have thoughtfully arranged some tables and chairs in a makeshift semblance of a classroom.

Mr. Robbins leans forward into the microphone at the guard station and his voice booms out over the loudspeakers. "Red square! Make sure your beds are stripped! Red square!" Red square was a reference to the painted block just in front of each cell door. Doors were being unlocked and the boys were to step out, stand on the red square, and await further instruction.

Fifteen doors open simultaneously and out of each one steps two boys. Some are rubbing the sleep out of their eyes, groggy from morning meds and breakfast. Others are pulling on sweatshirts and shoes still. Kids who I had never seen before, or who were supposed to be in the special day class for the severely emotionally disturbed, were coming out. Rival gang members, special ed, resource pullout, independent study; everyone is coming out.

The students are able to work without assistance for about ten seconds. Then hands began popping up like meerkats. I dash from one student to another, answering one question while five other voices asked for me help. There was only one of me and thirty of them. A good handful of them, the ones that were normally in the special education class, were clearly and completely overwhelmed by this assignment.

"I don't know what analyze means." A thin, blond curly haired boy with a lazy green eye and an upper lip that looks melted blocks my path with his long, scarred arm. I don't even know this kid's name. I have only seen him passing in the halls on the way to the special day class. Even under his sweatshirt, his shoulder blades are sharp as wings. He drags his fingers across the side of his neck, the skin gathering under his nails. "I hack military computers. I can break into anything."

I am not sure if this is a blatant lie or a statement of fact. Either way, it's an odd thing to tell someone within the first ten seconds of speaking with them. I give him a half nod of recognition. He rubs his ear against his shoulder, his right hand playing an invisible piano on the table.

"Miss Wehr, haven't you worn those same shoes two days in a row?" Jose was clearly irritated at the lack of attention he was receiving. Lately his attempts to redirect focus back to him have become more and more childlike. The other day he actually stomped his feet in frustration, fists balled at his side. He has done everything but tug at the hem at my shirt.

"Jose, haven't you worn that whole outfit for three weeks in a row? Now get back to work or you are going to get timed out." Some days your patience is an ocean, others it's a puddle that you stomp through without galoshes.

"Okay, okay," he grouses. "You don't have to give me an old tomato."

"I don't recall giving you any fruit, new or old."

"An old tomato! You know! When you tell someone they gotta do one thing or the other."

To save what shreds of sanity haven't yet jumped ship, I tell the boys to pair up with someone. Jose sidles up beside the military computer hacker, guessing that his wire-rimmed glasses make him a safe bet as a work partner. I can feel Hacker's eyes like a grease burn on the back of my neck. There is a gristly hunger in his face that makes my blood turn to dry ice.

"She is hella fine. I'm going to ask her out. She ain't a les, is she?" Hacker casts a glance at my boots.

"Nah, that's just the way she walks." Jose sighs, realizing that he has made a horrible partner choice here.

"I bet you a bag of Cheetos that I can get a date with her."

"You on, white boy! No way that's gonna happen."

At this point I have to cut in, trying to mask my amusement with feigned outrage. "Did you just barter me for a bag of Cheetos?"

"A bag of Hot Cheetos! You are worth it." Jose is overestimating his ability to flatter a woman out of outrage. He throws himself backwards into the aisle, legs sticking straight out like the world's most attention deficit two-by-four. "Miss Wehr, are you Republican or Dominican? Miss Wehr! Miss Wehr, it's not nice to ignore people when they are talking to you!"

"She's not here." I swerve around his big, grinning head.

"Yes, you is." He pitches forward, throwing himself onto the table and sticking his arms in my flight trajectory.

"No, I isn't. I have changed my name." I sidestep, doing a crossover move usually reserved for people wearing cowboy boots in western bars.

"What's the new one?"

"I'm not telling you," I call back over my shoulder as I round the table.

"You look like Peter Pan today."

Looking down, I realize that he is absolutely right. Between my green shirt, my skinny jeans, and my short boots, I am an easily passable leader of the Lost Boys. Fairly fitting, actually. The boys pull their sweatshirt sleeves over their hands with their pencils protruding, a la Captain Hook. Grinning, Jose throws his worksheet that he has torn into tiny pieces over my head, crowing, "You can fly!"

Sara comes into the unit, dragging a large cart of basketballs behind her. I have never in my life been so glad to see a PE teacher, not that there is much competition for that honorific. Stepping into the SMU unit next door, I am reminded on a myriad of levels that I am in baby prison. There is no artwork or motivational posters on the walls, as in other units. Shoes are outside of every cell door; the kids are not allowed to have their shoes in their single-bed rooms. Having a roommate is a privilege not allowed here. The boys are already out, seated at circular metal tables that are bolted to the floor, in backless seats that were soldered to the tables. Juan and Antonio are both on this unit temporarily as punishment for making pruno in their room, a glove full of rotting fruit and hand sanitizer having been found under a bunk during routine room checks.

"Hey guys! How are you doing today?" At this point faux enthusiasm is the only thing even vaguely masking the exhaustion and irritation that has taken root in every corner of me.

"We cool," Antonio grins, stretching his long arms above

his head.

"We cool? I feel like that sentence is missing a verb."

"Sorry. We be cool."

"We be cool?"

"Yea, like Toys 'R' Us. We 'B' cool. Why you always bugging us about grammar? Homies at the toy store don't even know how to spell and they're rich!"

"It's cause they got that giraffe," Juan says matter-of-factly.

In the corner of the unit a lone boy stands at his door, staring at me through the thin window. Wavy black hair down to his shoulders and deep brown eyes, he could have passed as Kevin's little brother. A blurred tattoo stretches across his thick neck. Knowing there is probably a good reason why he was not allowed out, I tuck my head down and avoid eye contact. A few minutes later, his face has changed into a contortion. His left eye is twitching, his mouth twisted into something primal and horrible.

Mr. Thompson circles the unit, peeking into windows for room checks. He stops abruptly at this door and yells at the boy, a single syllable of reprimand. He jogs back to the guard station, grabs a long sheet of green construction paper, returns to the cell and covers the window with it.

"You fucking bitch!" A screech comes from the room, followed by the dull thud of objects being thrown against the glass.

"He was watching you and masturbating," Mr. Thompson murmurs as he passes me.

I turn back to my students, trying not to betray my horror. Teenage boys and masturbation are not strangers to one another but how malfunctioning does the machine of your brain have to be to justify doing this within fifty feet of the object of your arousal? The boy continues to rage for a few minutes, yelling and throwing things, until his cell goes eerily quiet. There is something disturbing and wrong about the quiet, like earthquake weather. Mr. Thompson feels it too and walks to the boy's door, yelling into it. There is no response.

"Hey! I need some backup here!" Mr. Thompson calls to Mr. Robbins and Miss Berlin who are seated at the guard station.

They rush across the cellblock to the door. There is a buzzing sound and the door is yanked open. The boy hangs there, his sweatshirt tied around his neck, the other end looped around sink faucet. The guards push into his room, ripping the sweatshirt from around his neck and shoving his wrists into handcuffs. Mr. Robbins grabs his radio and yells, "Code! Get down!"

The boys throw down their pencils and drop to the floor, their arms folded above their heads. Mr. Robbins and Miss Berlin drag the boy from his room. The boy, writhing and twisting in their grasp like a panicked crocodile, is barely five feet tall, his eyes puffy from crying. He blinks at me, his mouth trembling. The two guards wrestle him out the door, the boy yowling and screeching.

"You need to collect all their pencils. This is a code so they need to go back to their rooms until staff gets Daniel to mental health," Mr. Thompson murmurs over my shoulder.

The boys jump to their feet and book it to their rooms, slamming their heavy metal doors behind them. A metallic click resounds throughout the unit as they are all bolted shut.

"Your first encounter with Daniel?" Mr. Thompson splits open a bag of sunflower seeds, offering me a handful. "He's kind of a legend around here. He is really damaged, poor guy. He is one of the youngest sex offenders we ever had. Started at twelve. He has been in and out for the past four years."

"He was a sex offender at twelve? Jesus."

"Well, he spent most of his childhood being molested. So he's very sexual. On the outs he keeps it under control by setting fires instead. He once tried to set his girlfriend on fire." Mr. Thompson spits shells into the trashcan. They stick to the plastic in clumps.

I felt my knees turning all gelatinous, the room a hellish merry-go-round. Mr. Thompson shoves a chair into the back of my knees. I fold sharply into it.

"But in here, he doesn't have access to matches so he acts out this way. We even have to put him in a cell that doesn't face the showers because it was making all the other kids really uncomfortable to be masturbation material while they showered every day." He opens his mouth a few more times, eel-like, but decides against saying anything else.

I have never been this close to a child so broken, ruptured like a blood vessel and leaking his pain into the fabric of life. What a desolation this is, what a wasteland. "So what can we do for him?"

"Nothing. We can't undo what happened to him. He will just spend the rest of his life in and out of institutions and jails." He cracks a seed between his yellowed teeth. It snaps like a bone.

"So it's hopeless?"

He wipes his hands on his black pants and swivels back to his computer for a moment before murmuring, "I can't think of another word for it."

*****

A front porch is a fabulous place to mull over a day's events with a glass of wine. Nothing in my graduate school experience had prepared me for today. Learning about severely damaged and hurt children out of a book does not prepare you for actually encountering one. The closest I had come to something so heartbreaking was last year during my student teaching.

I had instructed my students to write a poem. The topic was their own choosing. One of the girls in my class, a chipper, high-achieving seventh grader named Rachel had turned in a poem whose first line began with, "I am a suicidal girl." No thirteen-year-old's poem should touch on such a dark topic. Was this a cry for help or simply the emotive writings of a creative, albeit dark young lady?

I weighed the worst case outcomes of my options. If I reported her to the counselor and it was merely a poem with no insidious intent, then she would be upset with me. If I did not report it and it was indeed a cry for help, she may end up dead. I can deal with the silent treatment from a pissed off student. Knowing that a child has taken their own life and I did nothing to stop it was something I could not conceive of.

The next day I spoke to the school psychologist and Rachel was called into her office. She was in there for several hours, but made it to her last period English class with me. She walked in the door, eyes pink from crying and approached my desk. Standing before me, her hair half hiding her downcast face, she whispered, "I just want to say thank you."

I was not supposed to, but I stood up and wrapped my arms around her. Her body shook as she whispered, "I have been trying to ask for help for months. You were the first one that listened."

I pulled back from her, holding her at arms length, tears dripping down my face. The rest of the class was deadly quiet. A few of her friends, who I suspect had known for a while, wiped tears of their own away. Then with the kind of bravery that only a heroine possess, she lifted the black mane of hair from her neck, revealing deep red scars, stretching from her collarbone to her jaw, all self-inflicted, all in various stages of healing.

"I have been cutting for months." Rachel's voice was fine yet coarse, like steel wool. "The counselor told my mom and they are going to get me a good therapist." A watery smile broke through the storm of her beautiful face.

I will never forget the courage of that little girl. She will always be close to my heart and I will always wonder where she is and what wonderful things she is doing with her life. I was fortunate enough to be able to help Rachel. I listened to my gut. But what about Daniel? Had he ever reached out and been ignored? Could someone have saved him?

November 30

"Whatcha doing, Miss Wehr?" Antonio asks as the boys straggle in.

Perched precariously atop a rickety step stool I had stolen from the supply closet, I put the final piece of tape on a list of virtues I had stuck above the bulletin board. "We are bringing virtues back."

"Like Justin Timberlake?"

"No, sexy is not a virtue, although I am sure you would disagree with me on that. A virtue is a positive character trait, like honesty or responsibility."

"Or thugness. I want to be more like a thug. Thugness is my virtue," Jorge says.

"No, thugness is not a virtue. It's not even a word."

"Maybe it is for some people."

Deciding to start on a virtue that I have heard my kids discuss time and time again, we begin our dissection of love with a writing exercise about the ideal characteristics we would want in a partner. I am really hoping I don't get a bunch of papers that read like descriptions for Russian mail-order brides.

The timer dings and hands shoot up. I bask in this like a sun-soaked cat for a moment; this is the first time that hands have gone up across the board before mouths have opened. Jesus is waving his hand like he is trying to flag a taxi. I am trying unsuccessfully to force myself to like this kid, but it's about as effective as ordering someone to find you attractive.

He begins, "The qualities I most want in my bitch are…"

"Ummm." Now it's my turn to hold up my hand. "Sorry to disrupt your flow here but I am going to need you to find another word for bitch."

"My bad. The qualities I most want in my ho are…" He glances up at me and screeches to a halt. "Maybe I should change some more things and read at the end."

I expected to hear the boys ramble on about the more domestic traits: cooking ability, housekeeping skills, fecundity. The list of adjectives, however, is anything but shallow: respectful, honest, intelligent. The one that joined all their criteria lists is self-respect.

"Hold on a second. I just need to clarify something here. You guys all said that you would not marry a woman who sleeps around but you refer to women as sluts and whores and boast about how you use them and throw them away."

"We don't respect those girls. They don't care how they are treated so we don't have to try. It's like playing a kid's board game. You know you are going to win, no matter what," Jose explains. "How you treat a whore and how you treat a girl you like are different. Sluts expect to be treated badly. They don't care how they are treated."

"Yes, they do. They may act like they don't care, but they do. They have to act like they don't because their lives are filled with men like you who take what they want and throw the girl away."

"If a girl has self-respect, then we are going to treat her good," Marco says. "But if she doesn't care about herself, why should we? You know how to treat a girl by how she treats herself."

"Did you ever stop to think that a girl might have low self-respect because no one has ever treated her well? You don't have to date her, but for God's sake don't treat her like a piece of meat. Every girl is someone's daughter. What if someone treated your daughter the way you treated the last girl you slept with?"

The boys murmur angrily to one another for a moment, agreeing that anyone who would do something like that to a female they love deserves to lose an appendage. I stay out of it for a minute, letting them sit with the anger.

"I know what kind of a wife I want," Carlos says. "I want a wife like you. Do you have any younger friends, like around my age? Ones that you can bring here?"

"Since when do I bring you women? What are you, the Prince of Persia?"

"I don't know what that means, but if you bring me a woman, can you find me one that doesn't talk as much as you?"

"They all talk a lot. My girlfriend always wants to talk about why she is mad at me, which is like all the time." Juan seems fed up with my whole gender.

"Let's add one more part to this assignment, just a few sentences about who taught you how to treat a woman. What you learned from them and how it shaped you."

"You think just because you got us to write, you can keep piling on the work?" Jose smiles.

"It's terrible, isn't it? You should plead your case to Amnesty International."

Carlos's head pops up. "What's that? Can they bring me a woman?"

"I got it! I have something to say!" Jesus has laced his pencil through a hole in his paper and is waving the lined flag above his head. "Should I stand up? I kind of want to stand up. I am going to stand up. I learned how to treat a woman by watching my dad. He used to drink all the time and get mad and throw shit. Sometimes he would hit my mom and I had to stand in-between them. When I was nine, he broke my nose. Even when I was little, I knew that was wrong. So in a weird, backwards way my dad did teach me how to treat a woman." He drops back into his seat, the paper crumpled from where he has been clutching it to his heart as tight as a prayer.

December 1

"There's a baby bird that needs help!" Yvonne crows, bustling off towards the housing units, clutching a broom and a mesh bug catcher.

"Are you going to do some light cleaning before you help it?" asks Ralph.

"Smartass! It's to push the bird into this!" Yvonne shakes the butterfly hutch at us.

We are in the hallway again, waiting for the kids to come down. It is an almost daily routine. A few minutes before school starts, we congregate in the hallway and chat as we watch the kids proceed to school.

"I have to get to it before the guards spray it with Raid like they did with the baby bat they found."

"They sprayed a baby bat with Raid?"

"You think that just because they are adults, they automatically do the right thing?"

Sharon, who works with the more high functioning special education students, appears at my door. The woman is a whirlwind of serenity, despite constantly being pulled in five directions by her overwhelming caseload. Yet she always pauses to listen and maintains a chipper disposition. I have no idea how she does it.

"Can I have you send Eduardo down to me when he gets here? I have to do some reading tests with him." Her hair is wound into a loose bun around a pen, her thin hands partially obscured by the flowing pink linen of her top.

"Why do all the kids avoid Eduardo like the plague? What did he do to get in here?"

"I don't know." Sharon's thin lips are pursed tightly. This question is not one that she likes. "I don't want to know either. That's not our job, Hannah. That's probation's job. Our job is to teach, remember?"

I am a bit taken aback by the bite in her response. I have never heard her speak this sharply to anyone. "I'm sorry. I was just curious as to why the other kids are treating him so differently than they do other kids."

"I am not trying to bite your head off here. I find it's best to avoid any knowledge of the crimes our students have committed. Some of them will share, just because they want to talk. But once you know, it taints how you view the kid forever. They go from being John to being John the armed robber."

I hadn't thought of it that way. Would I be able to look at a kid the same way after finding out that he was here because he raped someone or tortured an animal or something equally horrific? Could I be totally impartial and not allow what I knew to affect how I acted? Honestly, I don't know that I could. By nature, I am prone to being judgmental. I make snap judgments on things, often without taking the time to really analyze the validity of my assumptions.

During lunchtime, Jack makes his daily changes to the student's grouping assignments. Every day students are released or transferred or admitted and the master school list is altered. Today, Jack's face is a mask of consternation as he glares at the clipboard. " I don't know where the hell to put Eduardo. He said he doesn't feel safe in the group he is in, but I get the feeling he is going to be harassed no matter where I put him."

"Why?" Yvonne asks, settling into her seat beside me with a big spinach salad.

"The kids in the other group were calling him a child molester."

"There any truth to that?"

"He is a blue dotter. I don't know much else aside from that."

A blue dotter is the nickname given to kids who are in for sexual crimes. A blue dot sticker is put on their folder to make them distinguishable from non-sexual crime cases. Before I began working with this population, I naively believed that only adults committed sexual crimes and that I would not have to deal with the perpetrators. But I guess every adult sexual predator has to start at some point. My mother, who has worked with incarcerated youth for years, reminded me that children who molest other children may be criminals in the eyes of the law, but they are also victims. No child becomes a sexual predator unless something similarly horrific has been done to them.

After lunch, Mr. Robbins stops to chat with Jack and myself in the hallway as we wait for the kids to come back to school.

"So I can't really find a good place to put Eduardo," Jack explains. "He is a Norteno so he has to stay with that group. Hopefully nothing bad will happen to him."

"Guy's going to get harassed as long as he is in here, no matter what group you put him in," Mr. Robbins sighs.

"Why is that? And can't you guys get him to take a shower?"

"This doesn't leave us," Mr. Robbins lowers his voice and leans in. "But Eduardo was a crack baby who was molested by his step dad in the shower when he was little. That's why he refuses to shower. At this point, it's been a week and he smells so bad we had to give him his own room. Well, have a good rest of the day!"

Mr. Robbins heads back up to the cellblocks, leaving Jack and I in stunned silence. Part of me wants to pity him because of what he went through and part of me wants to shun him because of what he did. Yes, he did something wrong. Something horrible and wrong, but he is still a child himself and one whose damaged childhood has left lasting repercussions on his psyche. I am not a lawyer or a jury or a probation officer. I am a teacher. And all of my students deserve the same amount of trust, patience, and education, regardless of their offense. Let the legal system deal with the infraction. I need to focus on the student, not the charges. It's a weird limbo to get emotionally close to a criminal. You see and resonate with and honor the human parts of them and try to either ignore or reform or understand the broken parts. Until I came to work here, my emotions have never overlapped so much. It's like having an octuplet Venn diagram for a heart.

December 8

If there is one thing that I loathe, it's people in positions of power who abuse the privileges bestowed upon them and unfairly treat those who have no voice. While most of the people who run the housing units are genuinely interested in rehabilitation and want the best for these teenagers, there are the few staff members whose intentions are somewhat questionable. Staff can be divided into two categories. There are those who keep the students out of their rooms as much as possible, organize game and movie nights, take the boys for walks around the grounds and trips to their vegetable garden to weed and water. The ones that I have had the most encounters with, like Mr. Robbins and Mr. Thompson, fall into the former. Then there are the ones who keep the kids locked up in their rooms as long as they legally can so that they can sit at the guard station playing solitaire on the computers. These are the staff that stand around outside my classroom door, loudly telling inappropriate jokes and yelling to each other about football scores while my students struggle to focus. Mr. Nelson and Mr. Walsh fall into that category. I have tried asking them to move away from my door or at least lower their voices and was met with looks sharp enough to cut a hair in half.

Our school offers GED testing for students as an alternative to a high school diploma. As educators, we want to reward students who pass their GED exams. Juan, who has been here for a year already, finally passed his exams. When he got the news from the GED proctor in my class, the other students burst into applause. Juan's smile was so immense that his head fell forward with the gravity of it.

During lunch break a few days ago Karen, the GED proctor, mentioned that she had promised to get Juan a bag of chips if he passed his GED. Students in here will do anything for a bag of Hot Cheetos. She added that she was also going to get mini bags of chips for the other boys on the unit to avoid any snack-related envy. I found this to be a very sweet gesture. Karen is a very pleasant woman, albeit it slightly jaded due to thirty years of working with this population. She has seen and heard it all and she is tired by it.

Junk food is extremely limited as the institution has very strict food rules so even something as small as a little bag of chips means a lot to these kids. All snacks that come from the teachers have to get the approval of one of the institution's managers and be given to the guards on the units, who will in turn give them to the students. Everything has to be individually sealed, nothing homemade, and nothing with chocolate or nuts to avoid allergic reactions. Chips in individual, hermetically sealed bags seemed like a snack that would pass from us to the guards to the students without an issue. However, this idea that we need to limit the junk food intake of our kids is pretty laughable when Hot Pockets, nachos, and cinnamon rolls qualify as acceptable, healthy meals.

Karen brought the bags of chips to school and we walked up to the unit to deliver them to the staff members. As we walked up the curved path to the first housing unit, we chatted about how glad the boys would be to get a treat. We were buzzed in through the door and approached the guard station where three large men sat, two texting on their phones and the other, Mr. Nelson, was eating French fries and watching something on the computer.

"I wanted to give these to you for the kids," Karen said, handing the chips to Mr. Nelson.

Mr. Nelson took the bag and shoved it silently under the desk. He would be the most attractive guy here if not for the complete wretchedness of his attitude. A form like a marble statue, with skin to match, he is physically arresting. His sharp blue eyes remain locked onto the computer screen in front of him. I glance at the pane of glass behind him to catch the reflection of whatever had so intensely captured his interest: solitaire.

"The big bag is for Juan. You know, for his GED. And the smaller bags are for the other boys." Karen's grin is almost painfully forced as she tried to maintain her usually pleasant disposition in the face of such blatant rudeness.

He nods but refuses to make eye contact. Is a word or two of acknowledgment really so taxing? We leave the unit a bit miffed, but still glad that the boys would soon be enjoying their snack.

Yesterday, Karen asked the boys how they had enjoyed their snacks and she was met by a classroom of confused faces. She put two and two together; the boys hadn't enjoyed their snacks.

They hadn't even been given their snacks. The guards had eaten every bag of chips.

Today we are teaching up on the units again because four guards had called in sick. Illness seems to strike very heavily on Fridays. At the end of first period, Mr. Nelson asks me to step into the program room with him. He shuts the door behind me.

"I don't know why you feel the need to run your mouth," he begins, his arms folded across his muscular chest. The fluorescent lights cause his shaved head to glow like the world's most ill-tempered angel. I must look confused because he continues, "I heard what you said about me."

Said about him? It takes me a second before I remember mentioning in the break room at lunch the other day that a friend of mine who used to work with him at another high school had mentioned he was fired for getting into a fight with a parent. My inquisition wasn't malicious, merely curious.

"Oh. I just wanted to know..." I begin, but he holds his hand up to indicate that he was not yet done speaking. I feel like a middle school student being reprimanded.

"I know what you are doing. And you don't know my business. I have a good reputation here and I am going to keep it that way. So next time you feel the need to run your mouth, I would think twice. I have been here six years and you have been here a few months."

I keep my mouth shut, nodding and maintaining eye contact, trying to pretend that I am not scared of this angry man. Behind him, I can see my students at the windows of their rooms, their faces creased with wonder and worry.

"I don't want us to have an issue." This is more of a statement than an opportunity for me to respond. I don't even know what I would say given the opportunity and it wouldn't change his mind. As Jack Kerouac said, *I don't know, I don't care, and it doesn't make any difference.*

Back in the break-room, I am blurry with fear and anger, tears rolling down my cheeks. Who had told him what I said? Why would someone feel the need to run over and gossip to him? From day one, the idea that there is them and us has been impressed upon me, both through the advice of some of my co-workers and also through observing our respective faction's interactions. To think that there was someone on my team who would spin and run and divulge like that. The thin bubbling layer atop my fright was betrayal, burning like acid. In Sunday School, our Bible teacher made us lick a rock of sulfur when we used the Lord's name in vain. That same bitter taste was in my mouth now.

Yvonne takes one look at my wet face, catches my arm and leads me to the file room, the one area in the school department that is not within the range of the cameras.

"Mr. Nelson cornered me and told me off. I didn't even..."

"That bully! He always does this. This is what he did to me years ago. He got me alone and went off on me. I guess his tactics haven't changed. He had no right to corner you like that. He just wants to scare you."

"Well, it worked." I wipe my eyes on my sleeve. Crying always reduces me to a five year old.

"Let's take a walk." She is already pulling on her jacket with one arm and shoving mine at me with the other.

"I don't want to." All I want to do is go hide in a bathroom stall until three o'clock and then drive home to Orange County. Gang members, I can deal with. Armed robbers, car-jackers, murderers: no problem. But bullies are fucking terrible.

"It's not an option. Come on. It will be good for you."

Outside the gray sky and light drizzle, paired with the circling crows, matches my mood perfectly. We walk around the compound, tracing the perimeter like a finger across a page.

"It is not a good idea to put too much trust in the people here. Don't get me wrong, they are nice, but not all of them can be trusted."

"Shit. I can't trust the adults and I am not supposed to trust the kids either."

"This is not the best slice of humanity. Jail doesn't attract the highest caliber of people."

"Well, I expected that from the kids, just not from the adults."

"A lot of the people who go into corrections were bullies. Or still are." We stop at the crest of a hill at the back of the property. Three deer are meandering among the chilled brown grass. They stop and raise their heads, following our progress along the fence. "There are some very compassionate people in corrections, but the balance seems more tilted into the red."

We reach the northwestern most corner of the property. The parking lot is jammed with cars, the front steps dotted with tired looking parents and lawyers in suits.

"Those who have power often abuse those in their charge for their own personal gratification. They were bullied as kids. Then they become bullies as adults. They seek out a job where they can manipulate and abuse those beneath them."

There is the dull thumping of fists on windows. Our boys are standing at them, smiling and waving, making goofy faces and flashing peace signs. Antonio waves manically at me from one, then pushes the corners of his mouth upwards with the tips of his fingers. And I understand then what they are doing: they are trying to cheer me up.

The last two periods fly by quickly, thankfully. I am not feeling a great deal of love for this place today. Mr. Nelson's voice reverberates down the hallway when it is time for the kids to go back to their cells at the end of last period. I am terrified to see him, unsure if he is done with me. Juan casts a raised eyebrow at my fist. Looking down, I am holding two halves of a pencil that was whole a minute ago.

"Guys! Let's go!" Mr. Nelson bellows from the doorway, deliberately avoiding my gaze.

"Mr. Nelson, what are we having for dinner?" Marco asks as he files past him.

"Barbecued ribs and chocolate cake for desert," Mr. Nelson sneers, his mouth stretching into a disturbing smile. The students smiled eagerly at this, believing him.

"Haha. No, you are getting tuna and carrot sticks."

Their young faces fall, disappointed and embarrassed. There is something inherently cruel and vicious in what he said. Mr. Nelson is enjoying taunting the boys with visions of food they will never have while they were in here. It is the grown up version of playing keep away with a smaller, weaker kid's backpack. The tactics are subtler, but the maliciousness is still there.

December 14

"You can't teach these kids Shakespeare!" Nikki laughs at the silliness of my query, dismissing it with a flip of her bony white hand.

"Why not? It's standard high school material. Most kids get some exposure to at least one of his plays."

"But these kids? Come on." She shakes her head and busies herself shuffling the papers on her desk. "No, just stick to the board approved curriculum."

"Why not these kids? They are just as smart as any other kid. Just because their writing and reading skills may be lacking, that doesn't means they are brain dead. And we already finished the book the board picked out. It was a sixth grade text. It took us five days to read it. So why not use this time to teach some Shakespeare?"

"It would just be too hard for them. We need to teach them things that they can relate to. The board has gone to great lengths to find an English curriculum program especially targeted to kids in court schools." She folds her hands in her lap, her eyebrow a peak of disdain.

"Like *The Afterlife*? Come on! A book about a Latino boy from the ghetto of Fresno that gets knifed in a club? Isn't there enough poverty and violence in their lives as it is? What's wrong with teaching them something new? Something out of their realm?"

"The board is not going to shell out money for more books. Money is tight for all districts in California right now." She has gone to the money tactic. I had anticipated she would and I am ready for it.

"Look, I will pay for the books myself. The board doesn't have to spend a penny."

Nikki studies me closely for a minute, her fingers a waxy steeply beneath her chin. I am the thorn in this woman's side, but it's not the first time I have been disliked by a boss. She can hate me all she wants, as long as she lets me do what I have to do for my kids.

"You are getting too close to this. You can't make it personal. Don't get too attached to the idea of what you want these kids to be. You will just be let down." Interesting advice coming from a woman who has worked here all of a month longer than I have. "But okay. If you want to do this, you can. But don't say I didn't warn you when it goes badly and you have a bunch of frustrated and confused kids on your hands."

"That's my job. To make them understand. If they don't, that's on me."

Nikki rises from her desk, sighing deeply, "Alright. You can start Shakespeare after we get back from Christmas break. But you are responsible for all expenses and they still need to read all of the other books on your curriculum list. You have any ideas what book you are going to do?"

"Thank you! I will get the books right away. I thought we would start out with *Romeo and Juliet*. And then *Julius Caesar*." I add the last bit quickly, sotto voce.

"What?! Hannah you said one book!"

"Bye! Thank you!" I haven't run out of a principal's office that fast since I was in seventh grade and I got in trouble for putting dissected frog parts in my friend's purse.

Passing through the sallyport, Karen glances down at my huge Barnes and Noble shopping bag. "What do you having in there?"

Grinning, I open the bag, revealing forty copies of Julius Caesar and Romeo and Juliet.

*****

"Hypothetical moral dilemma." I preface the writing prompt pitch.

"What's that mean?" Vanessa asks.

"Hypothetical means it didn't really happen. Moral dilemma means a problem or a situation where what is right and wrong isn't really clear."

"All of life is shades of gray," Alexa sagely muses from her perch in the corner of the room. She likes to take the seat flanked by as many walls as possible, feeling securest when no one can approach her from behind. She sits on the top of her seat, stick-like legs braided around one another.

"So there is this man. His wife is dying of cancer. He has no healthy insurance and no job and no savings. The medicine needed to save his wife is very expensive. He tries to raise the money for months. His wife gets sicker and sicker. Until finally he realizes that he has to get her that medicine in twenty-four hours or she will die. In a moment of desperation, he breaks into the pharmacy to steal it. The alarm goes off and the police arrest him. Now the question is: did he do the right thing?"

The girls are quiet, a few squirming uncomfortably in their seats. Some of them glance at Miranda, who has lowered her head.

"Did she get the medicine?" Her whisper is barely audible.

"It doesn't say."

"What do you mean it doesn't say?" Her voice is rising from softness to anger.

"I mean it doesn't say. I don't know. That's not the point. The dilemma is about his actions. Not whether or not the wife lived." I have missed something here, something massive and traumatic. There is a wound that this has reopened.

"I want to know if the wife lived." Her head is up now, her eyes blinking back tears. "I want to know if she dies or not. It matters. To me, it matters."

"God, let it go!" Vanessa is getting irritated. "What the hell difference does it make?"

"Well, my mom is dying of cancer, so if I could get a medicine to save her, it would make a hell of a fucking difference." Saying this sucks everything out of her and she takes a moment to fortify herself before she whispers, "My mom is all I have. And now I am losing her."

The girls are all respectfully silent, hanging on Miranda's every word. Her chin is resting on her chest, one hand furiously tearing the nails and cuticle remnants off the other. Blood begins to line her fingertips.

"And it's my fault. When I found out I was pregnant, I told her. And a week later she told me she had cancer. I made her sick. I just wanted to be with her, so I ran away from my group home. But when I went to the last place we were living at, she didn't live there any more. I didn't have any way to call her or find her. So I did a bunch of meth and I blacked out in an alley. I woke up in the hospital. They told me I lost my baby. Some homeless guy found me lying there, with blood everywhere. He carried me to the hospital. And when I woke up, my mom was there. They found her somehow and she came. She looked so tired and sick and she just stared at me. Like she didn't even know me. Or she did but she didn't want to."

"Well that's sad, but it's not your fault that your mom got sick." The edge in Vanessa's voice has softened and she is speaking patiently and deliberately. Being soft is the same thing as being weak to Vanessa so this is an uncharted limb she is creeping out onto.

"If I had just been a better daughter, and not caused her so much stress and sadness, maybe she wouldn't have gotten sick." Miranda wipes her nose with her bleeding hand, blood streaking her cheek like war paint.

"Your actions may have caused your mom stress. We have all caused our parents stress. But you did not make her sick. Don't think for one second that you made her sick. Getting cancer is just one of those awful and random things that happens to people." My words feel flat and metallic as they leave. What can I say? All the Language Arts training in the world and I would still not have the words for this.

Tessa storms into the room, waving a handful of medical paperwork at me. She sighs loudly and dramatically as she flops into a chair, waiting for someone to ask her why she was at the nurse's office. Incessantly chatty and extroverted to the point of being manic, Tessa is a brilliant young mind that has had nothing to sharpen itself on, save for the streets and a series of group homes, all of which she has run away from.

"What did they say?" Vanessa asks Tessa.

"I'm pregnant," Tessa announces, faux annoyance barely concealing her excitement.

"Lucky." Vanessa has been trying to get pregnant since she was fourteen and has miscarried two babies in the past year.

Miranda shuts her eyes completely, screwing her face tight as a pickle jar lid. She looks like a child trying to magically wish themselves out of a bad place, wrapping her arms around her head to give her a safe space in the horrible wideness of this.

"I'm going to have the baby in here and it's gonna be put with a family until I get out and get my shit together. I want my mom to take the baby, but my social worker said she can't until she completes a rehab program. I wish she could just get it together and help me out."

The curse of an English teacher is that you see the writing opportunities in everything, your brain constantly searching for prompts like a lighthouse that never goes dark. "We all have something we want to say to our parents and maybe we haven't have the courage or the strength. Would you ladies be up to doing that now? We each write a letter to a parent?"

Tessa is the only one who wants to share her writing. She wears her past and her pain like a badge of honor.

"Dear Daddy, I am sorry. I know that you always thought I was a fuck-up. I know you were mad at me when you died. It's been exactly one year today that you have been gone and I miss you so much. The family needs you to hold us together. We are not doing well. I am in here. Mom is back on drugs and the cops took away Katie and Lisa. I haven't seen them in almost a year. I think they are in a foster home now, but I don't know. I am pregnant. It's Deondre's. I know you didn't like him and you said that he would get me in trouble. The judge gave me a year in here. I have to give the baby to Child Services cause mom is too fucked up now to take care of anyone. Daddy, I need you here. I need you to tell me what to do. I am sorry that I was such a fuck-up daughter. I miss you so much it hurts to breath."

"Thank you." It felt like an empty thing to say, but it is all I had.

She nods, closing her notebook and laying her head down on her desk, eyes screwed shut. Miranda's head is also down, her bloody thumb in her mouth. She has filled a page front and back with hundreds of *I am sorrys*.

One of the more matronly guards, Miss Berlin, who Tessa refers to as mom since she has spent more time in jail with this woman than she has with her actual mother, puts her arms around Tessa. Tessa's face crumples and she turns into her arms. Miss Berlin pats her back and whispers soothing words, Tessa whimpering softly. Miss Berlin turns down the static screech of her hip radio and keeps hugging Tessa. Miranda has gone to an almost catatonic level, staring straight ahead at the wall with her cheek still flat on her page of apologies.

Nikki slips into the classroom, quietly settling into the empty chair behind my desk. She waves me to go on with my lesson. Pay no attention to the dragon in the corner.

Then he appears in the doorway. My breath catches in my throat. My heart rate accelerates and my palms go clammy. Mr. Nelson stands above and behind Nikki, watching me. I feel like an animal in a zoo. Nikki's behavior changes when she becomes aware of him. She starts to fuss with her necklace and her hair. She smiles up at him nervously a few times, finally asking, "Can I do anything for you?"

Leaning down, he whispers loudly enough for me to hear, "I could use a cup of coffee."

Please, no. Please let the woman who is supposed to be my mentor and role model say no to a guard's demand for coffee. Please let her tell him to go get his own fucking coffee. Please let this woman with a Ph.D who is leading a school refuse to fetch drinks for a guard like a cocktail waitress.

"Sure. Yes, I can do that. Coffee?" Nikki gets up quickly, smoothing her skirt around her hips, looking at the floor.

He smiles and slides into the chair she was just sitting in, hoisting one thick leg over the other. "I like my coffee with cream." He is staring at me as he says this.

"Ummm...how much? How much cream?" Nikki is backing out of the door, doing this weird half bow as she exits, like a geisha who has suddenly been reminded of her place.

Mr. Nelson reaches out, touching her wrist. "I want my coffee the color of my wife's skin."

Nikki's confused expression must match the one I know my face is currently making. How the hell are we supposed to know what his wife looks like?

She exits, her head nodding spastically like she is having a very localized seizure. Mr. Nelson turns his grin back to me, triumphant.

December 20

Friday we are once again teaching on the units, ostensibly because of the rain, but everything is bone dry and the sky is only the lightest shade of chinchilla gray.

"They just don't want to tell us that everyone called in sick again," laughs Yvonne.

She has a good point. It seems like most Fridays we are teaching on the units either due to imaginary bad weather or too many staff calling in sick. The staffing is kept to a bare minimum so if more than one or two people call in sick, the staff to kid ratio is dangerously shifted. This is a probation staffing issue, monetarily fueled of course. The lack of money has hit this institution from both sides. Guards are being let go or having their hours cut at an alarming rate.

The educational side of the institution and the probation side are in a constant state of battle. They ensure security, we provide education. We deal in different things for these kids. In an ideal world, a balance would be struck and the two sides would be less Capulet and Montague and more Rosencrantz and Guildenstern. We should be working together, helping each other out, ensuring the best for the kids in our charge. Instead, we bring our petty problems, our life-sized personalities, our egos to this place. We get offended, we gossip, we roll our eyes, we fall out of the mutually beneficial relationship that we ought to be maintaining. In the classroom there is the clear divide between them and us. They stay out in the hallway unless there is a fight or a kid needs to be removed and then their presence is very much welcome. The teachers stay in the classroom and we find a peaceful medium between the factions. But when we are on the units, we are painfully aware of the fact that we are in their house. There is no barrier between us and we bleed into each other.

The housing units are not at all conducive to teaching. The cellblocks are cavernous, two stories high with vaulted ceilings. The acoustics are wretched, with noises being amplified and rippling across the open spaces. There are pods of metal tables with attached steel stools scattered across the building. This set-up could work as a makeshift classroom except that they are surrounded by the cells. Kids who are kicked out of class are kept in their cells and their anger and outrage usually isn't quiet. Donkey-kicking the door, punching it and slamming it with their heads, combined with the threats and profanities being screamed out make every class come to a grinding halt. You try to wait it out for a minute or so, hoping the kid will get tired. Some of them do but some can go on intermittently for hours. It's impossible to hear what the kids in front of you are saying and equally impossible for them to hear you.

Since there are no white boards to write anything on, trying to explain an assignment is pretty much a lost cause. Some of the teachers just resort to packets and movies when we are on the cellblocks. Even if none of the kids are having nervous breakdown in their room, there are kids coming back from court and visits. They have to be searched with a hand held metal detector anytime they come back into the unit. The machine they use beeps loudly and shrilly and the kid who is coming back usually isn't too quiet either. If things have gone well, they are loud and boisterous, eager to share the good news. If things went poorly, they retreat to their cells to kick the door and scream out their frustrations.

There are also three to four guards on each unit, only some of which try to keep their voices down when we are teaching. Probation officers and mental health people are constantly streaming in and out, pulling kids from class and then returning them before class is done, but after the instructions have been painstakingly explained. The worst is when a kid gets released. They are of course exuberant, which is never a quiet emotion, and their departure elicits a variety of responses from the rest of the kids. The released teen's friends will all have to say good bye to him or her, hugging or shaking hands, wishing them well and telling them to say hi to so-and-so for them. The released teen's enemies will snarl and grouse, grumbling about how far away their release date is and how shitty it is to be here. Getting any of them to focus back on their work is damn near impossible.

Personality clashes and inconvenience aside, the thing that I loathe the most about teaching outside of my classroom is that the daily quick-writes that my students jot down in their journals, become almost impossible to do. It's a small activity, taking no more than 10-15 minutes. The students get three minutes to write at least five sentences. I try to pick topics that not only interest my students, but also help them to grow in character. Topics such as respect, honesty, forgiveness, and compassion are common underlying themes in our quick-writes. After the writing, everyone shares and this invariably leads into some amazing discussions. The ability to disagree respectfully, as well as consider the viewpoint of others, is not only an important language arts skill, but also a crucial tool for one's life.

This type of interaction is futile when teaching on the units. Since there are no boards to write on, all commands must be verbal, which makes presenting a complex persuasive prompt nearly impossible, especially for my English Language Learner and Special Education students who need all instructions in written form. My students love their quick-writes and they are getting more and more eager to share their thoughts and opinions as the months go by. But when they are seated a few feet from the guards on their units, they are noticeably less likely to share and discuss. I think the classroom environment is a sort of safe place for them. It feels like a school. And the units feel exactly like what they are: baby jail.

It does take more time, energy and resources to move a hundred kids down from their units to the school but damn it, these kids need a change of scenery. They are going to be locked up in their units all weekend. Their daily two minute walks from their units to their classrooms is the only change of scenery they get. And the scenery isn't even that great. There are no trees in here, apparently because of escape fears. The grass on the field is fake and the dirt patches that line the pathways to the cellblocks are only sparsely dotted with weeds and bedraggled shrubbery. It's not the fault of the guards of course; they are just doing what they told by the managers who must have some sound logic behind their reluctance to keep the kids out of school if it's overcast. Maybe the rain in Northern California is poisonous.

I have tried to make my classroom as comfortable and inviting as possible. This isn't an entirely altruistic crusade though. Since I am spending almost eight hours a day in there, I kind of need to like what I am looking at. My constant campaign for a class pet has been shot down numerous times, so the only source of non-incarcerated life that I can have in my classroom is plants. I have a row of various sized pots along the windowsill. These are a constant source of competition for the kids. They all vie to care for the plants, as having a task instills a sense of normalcy that their lives in here are lacking. Things as simple as watering a miniature rose bush, plucking the dead leaves and noticing which buds are beginning to open, lift these kids from their surroundings for a moment. The kids feel a sense of responsibility to these few pots of flowers and ferns, and are always quick to chastise me if they feel that the plants are thirsty or are in need of sunlight. Every week a student is selected to care for the plants. This is partly a privilege and partly a challenge. If that student gets in trouble, no one else is allowed to care for the plants.

Antonio has been one of my more meticulous plant caregivers. As soon as he walks into the class, he checks the water pitcher, then lines the plants up in one line on the windowsill. He carefully plucks the dead leaves, rotates the pots so that all sides of the plant had access to sun, then slowly pours water into each pot, keeping his finger in the soil to make sure he does not over-water.

Last week he went to court and was denied release. As a result, he became petulant and obstinate. He was kicked out of other classes four days in a row so I didn't see him for a while.

When he finally made it to class today, he walks straight to his plants and then turns sharply towards me, demanding, "What did you do to my plants?"

"Nothing. I haven't touched them."

"That's what I mean! They are all dry and wilting. Why didn't you take care of them?" He slowly crunches a dead leaf between his fingers, staring in sad awe at the brown fragments.

"That's your job." It's hard for me to say this, but I have to fight my urge to protect my students from every bad feeling.

"But I got in trouble. I couldn't be here." He dumps water into the pots desperately and it spills over the top, puddles of dirt-speckled water pooling on the windowsill. He dabs at it frantically with the sleeve of his sweatshirt.

"When you get in trouble, it's not only you that suffers. What you do affects others, Antonio. You're not an island, detached from everything else."

This is the closest we have ever stood to one another. I can see every small scar on his face and up close his eyes are so much older than the rest of his face. They are the eyes of someone who has lived seventy years in only seventeen.

"I couldn't be here! You could have saved them and you didn't! You let them die! They depended on you and you didn't protect them." Antonio clutches the crisp brown stems and petals to his chest, speaking to someone who is not in this room.

January 9

"Today we say sorry to someone we have hurt."

"I already said sorry last week. My lawyer made me," Juan says.

"I have never hurt anyone. So I don't have to do this, okay?" Kevin is waiting for me to confirm this. He will be waiting a hell of a long time. "I can write one, but I am not going to really mean it."

"Then look at this as an opportunity to practice your insincere apologies. You can either decide to get something out of this or maintain your sullenness in silence."

"I don't know what half those words mean, but you sound pissed, so okay." The boys are getting better at reading the green and I am getting better at whacking away their chip shots. I think we are both kind of glad to dispense with the preliminaries and get to work every day, but the boys need to put in at least a few minutes of being incorrigible before they can concede.

"I want to share!" Antonio's hand shoots up. "I would apologize to my mom. She cries whenever she has to come see me here. She is all by herself with the kids and she is just so tired. My siblings don't understand why I am not at home and my mom doesn't have the heart to tell them. She shows me the pictures they draw for me during our one-hour visits. Just looking at them hurts so goddamn much."

He takes a deep breath, pausing for composure. He lowers his head a bit further so his eyes are hidden from all of us. The room is silent as a mausoleum, every boy sharing in this experience with him. They were all connecting in their loss, the absence of something allowing room for the uniting presence of pain.

"I would also apologize to my dad. He was murdered and right before that, we got into a big fight because I got kicked out of school. He was disappointed and said he didn't want me to end up like him. Maybe if I hadn't gotten into trouble at school, he wouldn't have gone to see that guy he owed money to."

This is a common thread in my students writing. They take everyone's burdens, accepting responsibility for every bad thing that happens to their family. They see themselves as the lone sentinel standing between their loved ones and poverty, despair, death. Much of the time it is not an entirely unrealistic assumption, as many of them are the breadwinners in fatherless homes. Stealing and selling drugs, while not encouraged outright, puts food on the table for the little ones. As Henry II said in *The Lion in Winter*, "There's no point in asking if the air is any good if there is nothing else to breath."

"Last, I would apologize to my girl. She is pregnant and I am not there for her. She has to do everything by herself and I know she tries to be brave but I can tell she is scared. She is going to have our son in two months. I don't get out for five. So maybe I am the most sorry for my son. And he isn't even here yet." He lays the paper down like a body into a grave.

Writing apologies is not an activity I really expected them to embrace as just the act of saying sorry is so disdainful that my students, when forced to admit their wrongdoings, simply say 'my bad'. Sorry is just too heavy a word and it renders its deliverer beholden.

"Next, I am giving you twelve questions to answer about yourself, like an autobiography in bullet points."

"I don't want to answer any questions. Cops ask too many of those." Carlos grouses from the corner.

"Did you hear the world is going to end in a few days?" Marco is wearing his dictionary on his head, ever the dignified scholar.

"I did hear that, so we better get to work if we want to have our work done before the apocalypse."

"Doesn't that make you think about what's really important, what really matters?" Marco is gently pushing away the questions I am trying to lay on his desk, a mildly distracted cat with a dangling feather before his face.

"It really does, but you still have to answer the questions."

"Godammit," Marco sighs, throwing himself back into his seat so dramatically that his Webster's chapeau flies backwards and nails Carlos in the chest.

I explain that they can give as much or as little as they want to this assignment, with fragments and paragraphs equally acceptable. As I am asking them to go all archaeologist, excavating themselves and showing me the fossils, I am in no position to set standards on minimum size here. The fact that they are even agreeing to go down into the dig with me makes this a success already.

"I'm not sure about these questions on interests. I don't think mine are appropriate," Juan says.

I always have to have a back-up response for Juan because he usually smacks away the first request anyone makes of him. "That's fine. You can just share the appropriate ones then."

"That would leave me with like…eating."

Eduardo is seated in his corner of purgatory, staring at the questions in front of him. I take a seat beside him, giving him my best I-have-all-day face. "Have you written your answers in invisible ink or do you need some help getting started?"

"I don't remember anything about my childhood, except the bad parts. And they are nothing you would write about with markers." He stops, waiting to see if this is enough for me. I keep my seat and my silence. His top lip curls in for an instant, a sign that he is out of his comfort zone. His mouth is rimmed in blurred red like he has just eaten a popsicle. "I don't want to write about it, Miss Wehr. If I write about it, I have to look at it. And I don't want to look at my life."

I should have expected this response or something similar to it, anyways. If all my students had wonderful childhoods, they probably wouldn't be in juvenile hall. "What about the question about your heroes? Can you write about someone you look up to?"

"I don't have any heroes. There is no point. They all leave." He meets my gaze, challenging and begging me to contradict him. To tell him that not all the good ones leave, that sometimes they stay and they help and make things better and love you forever. *Everything was beautiful and nothing hurt*, Vonnegut's con trails against the pallid blue of our right now.

I wish I could give him this promise. It would be the sweetest lie I ever told, but I have to give him the truth, barbed and mangled and malignant as it may be. "I wish I could tell you this won't always be the case, but I love you too much to lie to you. People do leave us, no matter how we feel about them or how much we look up to them or need them. I just hope that one day someone will stay for you, Eduardo."

"Hope doesn't work. I lived on that shit for years." He rolls a green marker between his sinewy, tentacle fingers, the nails bitten down to bloody fragments. Sores are gathered in the crevices like barnacles, knuckles white and split as birch saplings.

He has lived too long in the shadow of loss and leaving, his life a city perpetually burning. Eduardo has waited for a hero for years. His father denied him before birth, his creation ushering in an era of rejection. Just his existence, even in its smallest form, was worth leaving. His mother has chosen drugs over him for years. Eduardo's life is less important than a lighter and a spoon, inferior to the contents of a kitchen junk drawer. Telling him to search for heroes outside of himself is not something he has the energy for anymore.

"They say if you want something done right you have to do it yourself. What about being your own hero? Creating a life that you are proud of?"

"I have done nothing that I am proud of. I don't really do good things. Nothing I do is worth being proud of."

It is here that I find him for a second. I am teaching the walking, breathing remnants of trauma. I can do nothing to fix what has been done to them. No book can erase the pain, no poem hold the weight of the memory. Can grammar take back beatings or sonnets erase nights spent under freeway underpasses? There is no paper strong enough to hold your father's footsteps as he walks out the door for the last time.

But I can't stay in this black hole with him; I have to swim to the edge, extend a hand and coax him towards me. "Can you write something of what you want your life to look like? Imagine you could go back and make it what you always needed it to be?"

His eyes flicker and flash with what I am asking him to do: to look up, to look out. If he says no, I have nothing. Titling his chin up slightly, he says, "Yes. Yes, I can do that."

He gives me a few jerky downward moments with his hand, indicating that he needs to be alone to do this. Wandering to the opposite end of the class, I drop into a seat beside Juan. His square, tan head rests against the stark white of the wall, a colored pencil hanging from his chapped lips like a purple cigarette.

"You remember being a teenager?" Juan is far away and contemplative. He is trying to find a handle in me to hold onto, something to connect to. I always thought I would be the one to try and find that in him. It never occurred to me that maybe he was trying to do the same thing this whole time.

"Yes, it's such a messed up time. Nothing makes sense, you don't know how you fit in anywhere, let alone who you even really are."

"Did you get in trouble?" He grins his question at me, pulling the pencil from his lips.

"All the time. I was always in detention or suspended. I even got kicked out of school. And that was nothing compared to the trouble I got into outside of school."

"How did you get past that? How did you not just get stuck there?" He looks at me like he is seeing the vanishing point in a landscape for the first time.

"You just grow out of it. I did. You will, too." As soon as I say this, I realize that I believe it. I have to. If I don't, I have absolutely no business being here.

"You think I will grow out of all this?" He looks less sure than I feel. He can't see the end of this road yet, but he keeps stumbling down it because it's the one he has always lived on.

"Yes, I do. The trick is surviving to the point where you are ready to leave it behind. It is quite a thing to survive yourself."

"Surviving is the hard part, Miss Wehr. I don't think people get how hard it is until they really have to fight for it." He looks at me for a second, his pupils swelling into dimes. There is a shift in gears between us. "Was your life every in danger when you were a teenager?"

His hand is out to me, after almost four months. This is the only rope bridge he can meet me on. It's terrifying to look down from here, but I meet him on it.

"A few times. I believed I was indestructible, immortal even. Not because I thought I couldn't die, but because I didn't care if I did."

"You ever get shot at?" His eyes are reading my face like lines of text. He requires proof that we both stood at the same precipice at some point, that we passed our trauma from hand to hand like a relay race.

"When I was sixteen, I had a gun held to my head." A man in a black sweatshirt, pressing the cold circle to my temple, asking my boyfriend *how much do you love her?* A memory like that is never more than a second or an inch from you, a hovering stranger in a crowded room who you are always turning around into.

Juan's sad smile is the echo of what a boy's should be, his fist gently tapping out a heartbeat on the whitewashed brick of the wall. "I can't remember the last time I walked down the street without thinking that this could be the last day of my life. I never feel safe, no matter where I am. My house got shot up twice last year. The only time I sleep hard is in here." He rolls his head in a semi-circle along the crest of his shoulders, the tan trunk of his neck bulging. The weight of this is too much for a sixteen-year-old. "What does it say about me that I feel better in a cell than I do in my bedroom?"

"I don't know that it says anything about you. Your neighborhood, maybe. Then again, none of us know how we would feel about someone else's experience until we walk a mile in their shoes."

Juan has gone glassy-eyed for a second, caught in a room that I can't get into. He snaps back, a bit unsure of what I just said. "Walked in my shoes? Why would you want my shoes? Do you need my shoes?" He is already leaning over to undo the Velcro straps on his white institution-issued sneakers. His recognition of what he believes is a need in me and his knee-jerk empathic response make my stomach turn over with adoration. No one who saw how quickly he leaned down to give me what he thought I needed could question the beauty of this boy's heart.

"No," I smile and hold my hand out to stop the unnecessary sacrifice. "It's an expression. It means to see life from someone else's point of view."

"Is that an example of an idiom?"

"Yes! Exactly! You were listening!" I probably shouldn't be as blown away by this as I am, but up until now part of me has always felt like I am just lecturing to myself. The fact that he not only listened but he also remembered, makes my heart go all post-transformation Grinch, bursting out of the frame.

"I listen more than people think. My mom doesn't think I listen to her because I never do what she tells me to. I do listen, I just always do what I want instead."

"That's every teen. Rebelling and trying to find yourself is part of growing up. I rebelled and I had nothing to rebel against. I had a good family, went to a nice school, lived in a safe neighborhood. But I could always find something to fight against if I looked hard enough."

"Shit, if I had all that, I wouldn't have anything to fight against. I could just relax and focus on school and my future. I wouldn't have to worry about stealing so we can pay the electric bill or wondering if the guy driving next to me wants to kill me." He runs a hand across his forehead which has gone damp, even though the room is almost frigid. He looks at me like he is caught between begging for mercy and bursting into tears. "My mom has to work two jobs. I have five siblings and my dad is in prison half the time. And when he's out he is on drugs, so he only makes shit worse. My whole family is in the gang or selling drugs. No one gives a fuck if I go to school. Actually, my mom likes it better when I don't cause I can go out and make money. How the hell am I going to survive all that?"

Both Juan and Eduardo share something in common, no matter how much they isolate from one another. They are both piecemealing themselves to me, waiting to see if I have the patience and dedication to put them back together. Maybe they are afraid that if they opened their hearts like a box, all the monsters that escaped would scare me away.

January 20

One of the more common misconceptions I have heard from people is that all incarcerated youth are on a set road. Incarcerated youth are far more human than most of society would care to believe. Their paths are not completely paved and when we assume that they are, we add roadblocks instead of providing detours. The demonization of juvenile delinquents is a social coping mechanism; once we have dehumanized these kids, subhuman treatment seems a fitting match.

My kids are my heroes; the mental strength and courage that they must have to wake up every day never ceases to astound me. Life in a cell with only a thin foam mattress, a sink, and a toilet seems such a horrible existence. I know that I would break down after the first hour, but many of my students are surviving in this for lengths of time ranging from two weeks to two years. The freedom to eat when hungry, shower for as long as you like, to go outside just because you want to see a tree, are all gone. The fact that they can still laugh and create beauty speaks volumes for their emotional strength. Then again, most of them cut their teeth on hardship. And it's not just the boys who are struggling to rise from the remnants of their disastrous childhoods.

"Girls, let's talk nature versus nurture."

"I don't want to talk about plants." Shawna is looking crossly at me out of the corner of her eye. Her probation officer informed her yesterday that she can't go home and she is being placed into foster care, so everything is irritating her at the moment.

"Not that kind of nature. Nature versus nurture is what we call the argument about what affects us and shapes us. Stuff happens to us, good and bad, but all of it changes us in some way. Nature is what we call the internal factors, like DNA, and nurture is our experiences and childhoods."

"I think nurture impacts us the most. I grew up with a lot of abuse and drugs and gang stuff. That's what my life has become today. If my parents didn't allow that stuff around me, I don't think I would be here today." Miranda is all glass, transparent and smudged in the places she has been handled too roughly.

"Why do you always have to play the victim?" Tessa snarls, massaging her expanding stomach. She has plumped out these past few months, partly due to the pregnancy and partly due to the stress eating that so many of our kids turn to when their normal coping mechanisms are not available to them. She resembles an undercooked gingerbread man more and more each day.

"I am not playing the victim. I just saw a lot when I was little and look how I turned out. I have friends who didn't see that shit and they are all in high school, going to prom and being cheerleaders, not ending up in juvie after they smoked so much meth that they blacked out and miscarried their baby in a fucking alley."

"I hate him," Tessa whispers bitterly, twisting her dozens of braids into knots around her small fists. "My step-dad, what he did to me, what I went through... that's what shaped me. The hell with nature and that sure wasn't any kind of nurture. Abuse shaped me. Where is the abuse option in that question?"

There is nothing that I could possibly say that would make anything better, nothing I can do to take back what has happened to her. This is like watching a robbery through the windows of a passing train.

"What about Fetal Alcohol Syndrome? Is that nature or nurture? Cause that's what I had." Shawna asks.

"I was born addicted to meth and alcohol," Miranda adds.

"Heroin." Alexa raises her hand like she is answering the world's sickest pop quiz.

I wish for arms as big as the universe so I could protect my kids from everyone and everything that could and had hurt them. My kids have been hurt before they even took their first breath. They were born branded with the choices of their mothers, already learning that their lives are inferior to a bottle or a baggie. When your protection is worth less than a 40 oz, it sends a pretty clear message. From the womb on out, they knew exactly how they deserved to be treated.

"I was raised by my uncles. They are all Nortenos," Juan says next period. "So it was nature and nurture that brought me where I am. My blood and my childhood was all gang shit. If I didn't join, it would be like I was turning my back on my family. I didn't have a choice."

"Man, you had a choice." Jorge rolls his eyes. Him and Juan have become more fractured as of late, snapping at each other like two cats in a sack.

"No, I really didn't. I was twelve and my uncles gave me an option. If I said no, I wouldn't have anywhere to live and they would turn their backs on me. Maybe it's sort of a choice, but it's not a hell of a good one."

"So? You were twelve. That's old enough to go out and hustle. You could have handled your own shit if you really didn't want to get involved in the life." Jorge is keeping the line taunt here, not allowing Juan the mercy of slack.

"But it wasn't just me I had to think about. Pops was in prison again and my mom was working two jobs and I have five younger siblings. Who else would take in a lady with six kids who was at work fifteen hours a day? Family was the only option we had."

"And they supported you, didn't they? All they asked for was loyalty and respect, homie." Jorge's fist pounds the desk with each sentence, his eyes gone black and feral. He is speaking from his deepest marrow. "That's your family. You owe them your life."

Juan answers so quietly, "And they got it." His writhing and flipping is subsiding, a hooked fish beginning to weaken on the hot wood of a dock.

"Would you be okay with your own son having to make that choice, Jorge?" I ask softly.

"My kid has to make his own choices," Jorge says. "No one is going to hold your hand all the time and protect you from everything."

"But isn't a parent's first and primary job to protect their kid?"

"Yea, when he is little. But when you get to be eleven or twelve, you are responsible for yourself," Juan interjects. He has remembered which side of the fence he promised to stay on. He does not look me in the eye when he says this.

Eleven. Fifth grade. What a thing it must be to be responsible for your whole life in elementary school. "That seems really young. How much of life did you understand at eleven?

You're not even in middle school."

"At eleven, I knew how to make money and how to hustle when I had to. I could make meals for my siblings and I knew how to deal with cops and social workers. I was already working for my uncle's landscaping business on the weekends, too."

"How did you have time for school and homework and friends and all that?" I ask.

Juan looks at me quizzically, as if I had just asked him a question that everyone should know the answer to. "Well, I didn't."

"Would you want your brothers to get involved in this?" It's a low blow on my part, but if this is going to connect, it has to be personal.

"If they make that choice." Juan's eyes click over to the left and lock, his mouth moving mechanically up and down like an automated carnival fortuneteller, telling you everything and nothing for only a quarter.

The commitment diatribe is not something I can hear from him again. It's so much sound and fury. "The hell with choices! Would you want that for them?"

"No." This one word cracks the surface of the room like a crème brûlée.

"But we are already part of it. We made that commitment." Jorge's stoicism is the cold, hard marble of a statue that has stood amidst everything and everyone that has fell around it for years.

"So you can't change your mind?"

"Hell no. We ain't no dropouts." Jorge's words fall without interception, the boys knowing better than to catch live grenades.

"So you think the only way to leave your gang honorably is through death?"

There are a few seconds of quiet, the boys staring at me with a certainty that tears down my spine like a comet. Their silence says everything. The thought of my boys who I love with an intensity I have never known losing their lives over a color is such a huge and horrific truth that a wave of nausea drops me into my chair.

"What's wrong?" Marco asks, concerned.

"What the hell do you think is wrong? You have all but said that your life is less important than a number and a neighborhood.

Some of you may end up dead before you hit eighteen because you think dropping out of a gang is a worse fate than ending up with a bullet in your head."

"Why do you care? You will always have more of us. Just because we go, it doesn't mean hundreds more won't take our place. You won't be out of a job." The skin around Jorge's eyes goes tight, his lips turning in slightly like a cornered dog about to bite.

"No one could ever take your place. Any of you, ever. And I am sorry that your gang makes you feel that way." Everything is falling out of me like a ripped trash bag. "You are not a solider with a hundred nameless people waiting behind you to take your place when you fall. You are not replaceable, not to me."

There is an anger in their eyes; they don't want to hear this. Believing that your life is just another in a row of dominoes that must fall on the way justifies laying down for the cause. I hold out my hands, wishing they held anything that meant something to my boys.

"Excuse me, Miss Wehr." Mr. Robbins is leaning into the classroom. "I am sorry but I have to take the guys back to the unit early. We are short-staffed and I only have an extra staff to walk them back for the next five minutes."

I am frustrated, but not as much as the first dozen times this has happened. The probation department is currently on a budget cutback and the first thing to get slashed is staff hours. The pencil block makes its slow procession up and down the aisles, returning to me with one empty hole.

"I am missing a pencil, guys."

The boys collectively groan. A missing pencil means strip-searching and if nothing turns up, the whole group goes into lockdown mode. In the corner, Jesus shifts nervously in his seat.

"If you took it, you are going to get burned," Juan hisses towards him. "I am not about to get strip searched. Drop the fucking pencil."

Mr. Robbins leans against the door-jam, irritated. He looks down at his watch and then up at Jesus.

"Okay, I am going to turn around and count to ten. If anyone has the pencil, drop it to the floor." I turn my back to the class and count to ten. When I turn back around, the pencil has magically appeared a foot in front of Jesus. Juan and Antonio glare at Jesus, but say nothing. My boys would never snitch on each other, no matter how angry they are.

Picking up the pencil, I can't help but snap at him, "That was a damn stupid thing to do. You have been with me for four months and you pull this crap? This is first day shit, man."

"You have no respect," Jose snarls at him, his eyes a dry thunderstorm over a prairie.

"Miss Wehr, don't worry about this. We will handle it." Juan speaks calmly, his eyes still glued to Jesus who looks more confused than scared.

They have not turned against one another like this before. Normally homies protect other homies. Something is happening here.

"We are taking the corner back," Juan says. He strides purposefully into the room with Jose and Marco flanking him. "We got you."

I am scared for a second. This could go one of two ways and one of those ends with bloodshed. I kneel down so I am at eye level, lowering my voice so Mr. Robbins doesn't hear me. "Please guys, it was just a pencil. He made a mistake. Don't make this a revenge thing."

"Nah, it's not a revenge thing. It's a respect thing. He disrespected you. We can't let that slide," Juan explains softly, but firmly.

"I appreciate this, but you don't have to fight my battles for me. I can handle this on my own."

"We know you can fight your own battles," Juan smiles. "But we look out for our friends and family."

"No offense, Juan, but I am just your teacher. I am not your friend."

"No offense, Miss Wehr, but you are not just our teacher. You are our family."

They are showing respect and acceptance in the only way they know how. Who am I to question what form this takes? We all turn to the door, waiting for Jesus to enter. Enter he does, casting nervous glances at the guys. Silently, he takes a seat in the front row, eyes lowered. There is a red mark on his cheek. Order, albeit a violent sort, has been restored. I am learning that the key to classroom management here is to have the shot callers of each group on your side, but also making it known that you control the shot callers.

"Well, good morning! Here's hoping we have a petty theft-free day. And it's going to be a fabulous one because we are going to start reading Shakespeare's *Romeo and Juliet.*"

I am met with a chorus of groans and eye-rolls the like of which I haven't seen since I told the boys they would have to write.

"That shit is boring." Jorge groans, throwing himself melodramatically over his desk. I refrain from asking him when he is trying out for the Traveling Shakespeare Theater Group. "Homie doesn't talk right. If that was the right way to talk, we would all be talking like that still."

I walk to the board and begin to write Shakespeare on the board. When they get like this, it's best to not feed into it. The driving force behind their complaints is usually more procrastination than genuine displeasure with what's being presented.

"Why do you act like we are regular high school kids? This shit is hard and we are in here. Why can't we do something easy?" Antonio has taken the baton from Jorge for the last leg of this.

"Because if we did easy stuff, I would get bored." I am not going to do this dance with him.

"One more question! Do you have a boyfriend?"

"We have gone over appropriate classroom topics before and I don't think that was one of them."

"Do you have a girlfriend?"

"Okay, we are done here. *Romeo and Juliet* focuses on two rival families: the Capulets and the Montagues."

"What's a rival family?" Kevin asks.

"Families that hate each other, like rival gangs. Two groups of people who don't like each other because they have always been told that they shouldn't."

"Like the Crips and the Bloods?" Antonio asks.

"Yes. Or like you guys and the Southerners."

There is some uncomfortable squirming. Their discomfort is a positive thing; it means they are listening.

"So they had gangs back then?" Jorge asks.

"I don't know if it was technically a gang, but the basic components were there. You had groups of people who did not like each other, committed crimes and caused problems in their city, and tried to kill each other. So it's vaguely the same."

"What's vaguely mean?"

Antonio yells from across the room, "I think it has something to do with lady parts."

"Getting back to the two families, it's important to point

out that they were very similar. The first line of the play is 'two families, both alike in dignity'. They have a lot in common, but instead of focusing on their similarities, they obsess about their differences."

"What makes them so different?" Jose pauses from folding his paper into an origami swan.

"Not much actually, aside from the last name. They are both powerful and wealthy and prideful."

"So why did they have beef with each other? If they had so much in common, you would think they would be tight," Carlos says.

"Why does any group hate another group? Usually it's because they are different in some small way and it's easier to hate what you don't understand instead of trying to figure it out. Let's look at the Northerners and the Southerners. You guys are all Latino, you come from the same state, you are proud of where you come from, and you are protective of your loved ones. Those are all great traits, but when you focus on the fact that he wears blue and you wear red, you lose sight of what you guys all share."

"So in a way, they were a lot like us. They had their family and their hood and they did what they had to do to protect that." Juan has his processing face on, brow furrowed with this new information.

"Exactly! Aside from the dialogue and the weapons, there are not many differences between the Montagues and the Northerners. You are both proud groups who have a loyalty to your own that can turn violent."

"How does it end?" Kevin asks.

"The book? Well, it ends with a lot of death."

"Sounds like our lives." This travels outwards across the desktops and heads, a ripple turned riptide.

"What do you guys think of when you hear the name Shakespeare?" I am met with a litany of synonyms for boring. "I though this way in high school, too. It wasn't until college that I really saw how amazing he is. I was never brave enough to tell my teacher that. You guys have a lot more courage than I did."

"So what made you change your mind?" Juan asks. Their interest is starting to percolate and I have to strengthen this moment.

"What makes something interesting to you? Think of every movie or song you like. What do they have in common?"

"Can I be honest or am I going to get in trouble?" Jesus ventures cautiously. The boys' heads snap towards him, eyes flashing warning signs. I almost feel bad for Jesus at this point; it's like even his own homies have put him on probation. "I like movies where people get blown up or girls get naked."

"Sex and violence are definitely major selling points in cinema and music. But did you know that these were the same selling points Shakespeare used to get people into his plays?"

"I never heard any sex or violence in a Shakespeare play," Jorge pipes up from the corner, his arms folded across his chest.

"How many Shakespeare plays you read, homie?" Juan asks him, a tinge of irritation in his voice. Jorge clicks his tongue in disgust at this question, raising the back of his hand at Juan.

"I am not surprised you couldn't find it. It's there, but it's in code."

"Code? Why the hell would he use code? The way he talked is hard enough to understand." Antonio stops spinning the pencil in his fingers.

"Same thing as slang. You guys use slang all day, every day. Why?"

"It's just how we talk."

"But why use words that some people don't understand?" I ask.

"People use slang because they don't want outsiders knowing something," Juan says. "Slang stays in a group, so maybe it makes the group feel stronger. It keeps outsiders outside."

"Makes the walls stronger," Antonio nods.

"So Shakespeare uses slang to keep some information secret and to let others in on the more scandalous shit?" Jose's knee is bouncing furiously under his desk. "What's the point of that?"

"Maybe he thought he would get in trouble if he wrote about something that was not appropriate," Marco muses softly.

"In trouble? Like with the cops? Did they have cops back then?" Kevin asks.

"They had laws and people who were paid to enforce them, but it wasn't like the police force we had today. Cops aside, who was the other really powerful group in England a few hundred years ago?"

The boys rattle off a dozen or so theories ranging from drug dealers to women to the Illuminati before Antonio smiles knowingly, "The church."

"And what issues would the church have with what we just talking about?"

"The church would not be okay with all the sex and violence," Juan speaks slowly. "But why would the church even be involved in this at all? It's not like the plays were being performed in an actual church."

"Maybe the church was getting a cut or something. Like in exchange for letting the plays be put on, they got to decide what could be performed," Antonio says.

"The church definitely had a strong hold on what was going on back then. This was before the whole separation of church and state. Back to our original question: why would Shakespeare put sexual jokes and violence into his plays at all?"

"To get your attention!" Jose blurts out. "To make you want to watch more!"

"So, if I start my play off with a long talk about politics, what would most people do?"

"They would leave. So he put sex and fighting into the beginning of his plays to get people interested? Is that it? Did we figure it out?" Marco has tipped his desk forward onto its front legs, his excitement throwing him off balance.

"You guys figured it out perfectly. That's what made me change my mind about his plays. Once a teacher told me that, it became a game for me to read his plays and find where he hid the scandalous stuff."

"Can we start the play now?" Kevin asks, flipping rapidly through his copy.

January 27

"Miss Wehr! I got something for you!" Jesus crows, sauntering over to my desk.

I eye him skeptically. This is, after all, the same kid who after being lectured by me last week about not finishing his classwork, drew a picture of himself shooting me in the head.

"Another piece of art?"

"No, seriously." He lifts up his sweatshirt, revealing three books tucked into the waistband of his pants.

"I don't remember a Barnes and Noble being installed in juvie. Where did you get these books?"

"I got them from the library," he says, pulling the books out of his pants and laying them on my desk. A car maintenance manual, *Twilight*, and a book on teen pregnancy in Spanish. He knows me so well.

"You got them? Define got."

"I took them." He shrugs, shifting from foot to foot. He is starting to realize that maybe this gift was not such a good idea.

"You took them or checked them out the right way?"

His mouths twists into a spiral. He would not have books stuffed into his pants if he had obtained them to proper way. "I just took them."

"Why didn't you just check them out the right way?"

"I dunno. It seemed easier to just take them."

"Do you think you made a wise choice?"

"Taking them, yea. Showing you, maybe not." He skulks towards the door, shoulders drooping under the weight of his miscalculation. At the doorway he stops, shakes a pant leg, and two more books come tumbling out.

Today's last class is a bittersweet one. Antonio is being released in a week. Although we got off to a rough start due to our personality clashes that turned out just to be similarities bumping heads, he is one of my favorite students. His presence in my class is always such a pleasant one. Intelligent, articulate, pensive, and observant, he is the sort of student that any teacher would be lucky to have in their class. Most students are hyper and distracted as their release date looms closer, their minds already outside these walls. I expect Antonio to be the same way, especially since he had been in here for so long. But today he is quiet and reflective, removed from the rest of the students.

He stars at the white walls, blinking slowly. He is being released on probation, meaning he would be walking on thin ice with hot blades. Something as small as coming home a few minutes after curfew could send him right back to jail. He is going back to the neighborhood that helped him get locked up in the first place. He will live on the same street, hang out with the same people, and statistically speaking, probably end up in the same predicament within a few months.

I can't imagine the weight of knowing that although you are about to be free, your freedom is pretty much temporary as the slightest slip-up would send you back to jail. The stress of that knowledge alone would make turning to illegal distractions that much more tempting.

I try to lighten up the mood by having the kids write about their favorite food. The one thing that is pretty much universal among teenage boys is their voracious appetites. Incarcerated juveniles are even more consistently preoccupied with food. Being unable to enjoy a favorite meal is a loss even more pronounced by the sub-par cuisine offered up in juvenile detention centers. Life in here seems to center around meals. As soon as lunch is done, the kids want to know what they will have for dinner. It's comforting, I suppose. The act of feeding is soothing and maybe one of the few normalities they have left in juvie. The kids complain about most of the food in here though, with a few exceptions. They have rated the hummus as the worst food item and the nachos and popcorn chicken tie for the best. I have heard stories about stale bread, cold meat, unidentifiable mystery dishes. There have been meals that have sent my students running from my classroom to the bathroom. It's safe to say that juvenile hall won't be winning any Michelin stars anytime soon.

I try to remind the kids when they complain about the quality of the food in jail to use that displeasure as an impetus to stay out of here. Having to eat the same institution-manufactured, reheated/ microwaved food every day would be reason enough for me to never want to set foot again in a house of corrections. But the ones that worry me are the boys who love the food. Some say it is much better than the Top Ramen they eat three meals a day on the outs because that is all their family can afford and others are just happy to be eating every day.

I ask them to write about the best meal they ever ate and set the timer for the customary three minutes. When the timer dings, Juan asks, "Can I have more time to write?"

"Yea, me too," echoes Carlos. "Just a couple more minutes."

"You want more time to write?" I could be a stunt double for a large mouth bass at the moment.

Every hand in the class shoots up when it comes time to share. The list of foods they love is beautifully diverse. Everything from traditional Mexican dishes like enchiladas verde and tamales to junky comfort food like fried chicken and macaroni and cheese. They reminisce about their grandmother's posole and longaniza, biscuits and gravy, spaghetti and meatballs.

"The best meal I ever had was at Jack in the Box. Double bacon cheeseburger with fries," Jesus reads from his journal.

A few of the boys laugh out loud. Jesus looks confused, then embarrassed.

"Jack in the Box? That's not a best meal," chuckles Juan. "That's what you eat when you got the munchies."

"Think about what your mom made for Thanksgiving or what your grandma cooks for you," Antonio prompts, trying to be helpful.

"My mom works two jobs. I never see her. The only time I ever get food that's not fast food is when I am locked up, " Jesus murmurs.

"So nobody ever made you dinner?" Kevin asks curiously.

"I was going with this girl for a while and she would cook. She always used to laugh because I would just watch her. It was always so weird to watch her put stuff together in pots and pans and have it turn into something really good."

I originally planned to get into prepositions with the students but this moment of sharing and laughing and remembering happier times with family seems much more important. An exercise that usually took no more than fifteen minutes stretched into the whole forty-five minute period. You have to know when to just let things ride, I suppose.

February 1

"Everybody dies!" Juan and Jose are standing angrily above me. Juan waves his copy of *Romeo and Juliet* in my face. "In the book! Everybody dies!"

"You were only supposed to read the first act for homework."

"Well, we read all of it," Jose tosses his book down on my desk. The next wave of boys come in, clutching their copies and looking equally upset.

"Did you guys read the whole thing?" I ask them. They glare at me in lieu of a response.

"You didn't tell us everyone dies!" Antonio grumbles.

"Well, you don't ruin the ending. That's just not right."

"It's not right that they died."

They are silent, sullen. Some of them are glaring at me, and others at the book. They are not sure who is responsible for all this literary homicide: Shakespeare for writing it or me for assigning it.

"So what's he trying to say? That everyone who gets involved with the game gets killed? That what he's saying?" Juan is searching my face for something I can't ever give him.

"Is that the message you got from the book?"

"Well, everyone dies. Romeo and his girl and Mercutio and Tybalt. All they were doing was standing up for love and family. It ain't right that he let that happen. Just because we are in the game, that don't mean we are gonna die," Jesus says. I wonder who he is trying to convince.

"I didn't say it was." I hold my hands up as if being held at gunpoint. My boys are definitely more firing squad than student body right now.

"But you picked this book. You picked it for us to read. You did that because you want us to think that we are all gonna die," Jorge insists. "You think like everyone else thinks. That all gang members will end up getting killed."

"Jorge, you don't know what I think anymore than I know what you think. I hope that what happened to the characters in this book don't happen to any of you. I chose this book because it is a powerful and important book. If you saw something of yourself or your life in it, that's wonderful."

"How is that wonderful? I couldn't sleep last night. It made me mad," Jose says.

"It's wonderful when we can see any part of ourselves in any literary character. If it's a good thing, we can enjoy that. If it's a bad thing, we can learn from it."

"What am I supposed to learn from this?" Jorge shakes his book at me.

"Whatever you did learn from it."

"I didn't learn nothing." He tosses the book down and crosses his arms.

"I did." Juan takes a deep shaky breath. "And this might be wrong. But I felt like Shakespeare was trying to say that you can think something is right. You can feel it in your heart, but it could be wrong. Like sometimes you can feel something so much that common sense doesn't come to you. You are all in the...what is it...the heat of the moment! You are in the heat of the moment and it can feel right, but afterwards maybe you change your mind."

"What are you saying, blood?" Jorge has spun back around and is glaring intently at Juan.

"Haven't you ever thought about something one way and then after you think different?"

"Nah, homie. I keep it real. Nobody gonna catch me slipping."

"This isn't about slipping! It's about learning from your mistakes. Doing shit and then thinking that maybe you were thinking with your heart and not your head."

"I know what I did wrong. I don't need no book to tell me what I did wrong. I ain't scared for shit! The game is my life and I ain't gonna die like a punk!"

"But don't you get that's what Shakespeare is saying? If you aren't scared, if you just do shit without thinking about the consequences, then you will get smoked! Being scared isn't slipping! Changing your mind about your life isn't slipping! Acting without thinking, that's slipping!"

The more defensive the boys get, the worse their language gets. The tone in the room is tilting like a carnival ride. Eduardo is biting his nails and Antonio has shifted his grip on his pencil so it is being held like a switchblade. Mr. Thompson is standing now, his eyes darting back and forth between Jorge and Juan.

I take a step forward, holding my hand up. Jorge and Juan quiet and turn towards me, their cheeks red and chests heaving. "I just want to say how impressed I am by how deeply you have analyzed Shakespeare's message. He would be proud of you both. I know that I am."

"You aren't mad?" Juan looks confused.

"Why would I be mad? You expressed yourself using words. You just had a disagreement with someone and not once did you raise your hand in anger. You spoke out the fire in you and you did it with respect."

"Wow. We did do that, didn't we?" Juan's smile is the most beautiful thing I have ever seen. His cheeks look like they are about to crack open with pride. He leans forward and grabs Jorge's shoulders happily. Even Jorge, who moments ago looked like a bull in a ring, breaks into a grin.

February 9

It started out as a writing prompt: *Write about someone who has been taken from you or changed by drugs and alcohol.* I had meant this morning's prompt to be a warm-up exercise, taking no more than ten minutes or so. I had set the timer and watched. They were slow to start. Some of their shoulders had drooped under the weight of this. But they took a collective deep breath and dove in. I threw the timer in the drawer and just sat silently with them in this. They needed nothing but my presence, occasionally glancing up to make sure that I was still there with them before they took a breath and submerged again, the safety boat floating just outside of arm's reach of the channel swimmers.

Dear Dad, I haven't seen you for four years, but it still hurts me to know that you are a dope fiend. It hurts to hear people talk about you and say that I am going to end up just like you. I hate you and mom and you guys know why. - Shawna

When I was little I searched for someone to look up to. I wanted to know who mom and dad and sister were. I called you guys that as if that is what you really were, but I didn't really know you at all. When I needed you the most, to cry to or talk to, or tell me that I was loved and wanted, you guys were all out getting high and drunk. Even when I was around all the other little kids, I was still alone. I hated what a hold drugs had on you and I promised myself back then that I would never let drugs have me that way. Now I am so in love with drugs, I can't imagine my life without them. My life is a nightmare with or without them. But unlike you, they have always been here for me. -Jose

Drugs were an escape from my dad and all the other disgusting men in my life. I will never trust a man, but I have always put my faith in drugs. -Alexa

Dear Mom, I admire all of the times you tried to stop poking that needle into your arm. My earliest memory is being five years old and crying over your body in the bathroom, not knowing if you were going to wake up. Now you are in prison. They say you will be in for six years. I keep hoping that one day love will be more powerful than heroin, but I don't know if it ever will be. -Eduardo

Dear Brother, Because of you, I started doing coke when I was eleven. I never understood why my friends didn't do drugs with their big brothers, too. When I was thirteen, I tried to kill my mom and little brother because they didn't want me to do drugs. I want to kill everyone who doesn't let me do drugs.-Jesus

Hey Mom, your drug abuse has affected me a lot. You have not been in my life since I was a baby. I will always love you, but I won't talk to you until you get clean. I keep waiting for the day when you will choose me over meth. -Kevin

My dad has been using drugs since I was a baby. He left when I was two and my mom had to raise all six of us kids. Now my two brothers and me are in the hall. I wonder if my dad even knows. Or if he would care. —Carlos

Dear Mom, you lost me to meth. You said it was the cops that took me from you and I used to believe that. Now I know it was the meth that took me from you. Last time we talked, you said you were clean, but I don't trust you anymore. I want to, but I had so many scary moments as a kid when you were using. I haven't seen you since I was eight. It's been seven years. Now I am addicted to drugs, too. I am becoming you and it scares the fuck out of me. - Marco

Dad, I remember all the adventures that you took us on that were actually drug buying trips in disguise. I remember the cold nights of sleeping in your van and showering in the sink in gas station bathrooms. I remember the things that we had, all vanishing like a magician's trick, to support your habit. By the time I was five, I knew more about heroin and meth than any kid should. -Jorge

Dear Me, you have been in and out of juvie, rehab, and mental institutions. You have ruined your body, mind, and life with drugs and booze. You keep saying you will change but you throw it all away just because life is hard. Get your life together. I am addicted to alcohol. Sometimes I think it's bad because my dad drank a lot of alcohol until his liver stopped working and he died. One day he was alive and the next day he was dead. I think that will be me one day. -Miranda

My dad is an alcoholic. He says he is going to stop a lot but he always goes back to it at some point. Sometimes he doesn't do the things that an adult is supposed to do. Then I am left with his responsibilities. Sometimes it's like he isn't my father, more like my brother. My dad used to also do a lot of drugs. My
156

mom would get mad at him and they would fight. He used to spend the nights sleeping on the streets like a bum. I needed a dad to teach me how to act, but I never had one. Maybe that's why I am such a fuck-up.-Juan

I know this kid who lost his dad to drugs. The kid started stealing from his dad and coming home so drugged up that he would start hitting his dad. This kid's father was killed for stiffing a drug dealer. I am that kid.-Antonio

Dear Mom, when you were pregnant with me, you were so happy to have another baby. That's what you told me when I was old enough to understand. So what I never understood was why you drank when you were pregnant with me. You corrupted me from the day I was born, when the doctor said I had Fetal Alcohol Syndrome. If you really loved me, the least you could have done was stop drinking. But instead you kept drinking until it killed you. Now I drink away my problems too. It's the only thing you left behind for me. - Vanessa

After reading the last journal in the stack, I slipped it back into my school bag, laid my head down on my desk, and wept.

February 23

Every month our class focuses on a different virtue. The virtue of the month is discussed, analyzed, written about, and preserved in various forms of art. In honor of the month of February, the students are writing about love and then drawing a poster showing how someone can demonstrate this.

Colored pencils were passed out, classical music was turned on, and the students dove into their writing and drawing. There is nothing more satisfying than watching a class full of students giving their all to an assignment and enjoying it to boot. Their legs swing happily as they write and color their posters, the little kid in each of them wriggling in contentment.

This is definitely a much easier virtue for the kids to illustrate than last month's virtue, respect. When asked for an example of how he showed respect to others, Jesus thought for a moment before saying, "I showed respect to this one guy by not shooting him after I took his wallet."

I blinked at him for a moment, waiting for him to say he was kidding. Then I remembered where I was. "You are just like Ghandi, if Ghandi was a gangbanger."

In the back corner desk Juan stares at his paper, colored pencils still bound up.

"You stuck?" I ask, sitting next to him. Some of my students get defensive when you ask them questions while standing above them.

"I don't know what to write about love."

"Well what comes to mind when you think about love? Girlfriend? Family? Siblings?"

"I don't have any room in my heart for love. It's too full of blood." The poetry and the profoundness hits like an uppercut. His heart is so full of violence and loss and his gang that nothing else can fit in there.

I wonder what love looks like for my kids. A lot of them grew up in homes where women put up with abuse in the name of love. They learned that love means putting up with awful things. Some of their parents left, through drugs or incarceration, and they still loved them. Which makes it less baffling that they would mistake the acceptance of a gang as a form of love. When their homies do awful things and encourage them to as well, it's okay because they say they love you. It's like saying you love someone means that your behavior must be accepted. If you don't tolerate the abuse, you must not love that person back. Love is something that uses you, warping and bending you into a tool. Love is a liability.

*****

Part of working with this population is understanding that as their teacher, you must expose your students to as much of the world as you can. The majority of my students have never left Northern California. Some have never left their city. The idea of travel, learning about other cultures, immersing themselves in something totally foreign is just not something that occurs to them. They have no resources with which to make this happen, so why bother thinking about it?

It has been a pipe dream of mine for years to establish a non-profit that pays for at-risk/ post-risk kids to spend a year or two in a foreign country. The kids would be assigned a host family with whom they would reside. They would attend school, learn about a new culture, adopt a new language, and experience a completely new part of the world. I know that most of my students, if not returned to the same neighborhood, temptations, friends, and circumstances that got them locked up in the first place, would probably not reoffend. Take a teenage gangbanger out of his hood and away from his homies and what do you have? You have a teenager. Put him in a new neighborhood with a stable family, provide him with a strong education, and the once in a lifetime opportunity to immerse himself in a new lifestyle, and he will return home changed.

My students talk about defending their neighborhoods with the vehemence and zeal that we reserve for human rights violations and terrorism. I guess when you have never left the city you were born in, it can essentially become your world. It is all that you feel that you have and it is certainly all that you know. And these kids protect their neighborhoods against rival gang attacks the same way most people would protect the earth from an alien invasion.

As I type this, the clock clicks over to three in the morning. My eyes sting against the glow of my laptop screen. How do I bring a hundred locked up teenagers to another country? How do I let them experience another culture without leaving the classroom? Stumped, I get up for a glass of water and trip over a photo album of my trip to South Africa. I realize what needs to happen; my class needs to sponsor a child in another country.

March 5

The wallet-sized photo of Darwin that the international child sponsorship had sent me could have been the second grade school photo of any of my boys. Buzzed brown hair and big hazel eyes, he was wearing a V-neck sweater that had seen better days, his mouth parted slightly as if he was learning how to smile.

"So we are sponsoring him? Like all of us?" Jose looks panicked, the way he does whenever he feels something is being asked of him.

"I don't have any money," Jorge says. "How do you know it's not a scam? They could be just taking the money and not giving any to the kids."

"Does this mean we have to write more? Why do you make us write so much? Why can't we watch a movie?" Carlos has just returned from court. He got three more months and is in a wretched mood.

I fold my arms across my chest and purse my lips tightly until the boys go silent. "Yes, we are all sponsoring him. I am the one who is making the donations, all you guys have to do is write him a letter.The organization is very well known, so I doubt there is a scam being run here. And for the last time this is English class and we write a lot in English class."

"Miss Wehr, we are going to get purple funnel syndrome from all this writing," Jesus whines.

"It's Carpal Tunnel Syndrome and you can send me your medical bills."

"I don't want to have to take care of someone else. I can barely take care of myself," Marco says, shaking his head.

"We aren't taking care of him, Marco!" Juan exclaims, barely containing his exasperation. Juan has five siblings under the age of eight so he is used to having to explain things. His patience is one of his strongest virtues, long continuing even after mine has run out. "We are helping him. We write him a letter and he writes us one. We can talk to someone in a different country and he can practice his writing. Stop being so negative."

"Does he know about us? Like did you tell him we are in juvenile hall?" Kevin asks.

I tell the boys that I hadn't mentioned it, but if they want to tell him they are welcome to. Maybe they can give him some advice about what choices he should avoid making and tell him things that they wish they would have known when they were younger.

"I don't think we should tell him where we are," Eduardo whispers. Every head spins towards him. The person who speaks infrequently commands instant attention when they do. "This is nothing to be proud of and it's nothing that a little kid should know about."

"But it's the truth! It's our truth. We are locked up," Juan says calmly. "And maybe if we tell him not to do certain things, we can help him out. Nothing wrong with helping a kid out, man."

"Kids shouldn't know about bad places like jail. He is supposed to have fun and play and go to school. He doesn't need to know the bad things yet. Life is going to show him enough bad things." Eduardo voice falters and stumbles as he speaks, like a foal rising from the straw of his mother's stall for the first time.

"But that's the point, man. If we tell him about the bad things, then we can help him. We can protect him a little and keep him from making some of the mistakes we did."

"Why should we give this kid an advantage we never had?" Eduardo's voice is the creak of every door that has remained closed for too long.

"Is that how you see life?" Juan looks at Eduardo with a look of disgust and pity. "Like a fucking score? I don't know if you have been keeping track but we are all on the same team here. We are all people. We need to help each other. And if you can't see that, maybe it's better that you just keep quiet."

March 11

It's human nature to have a morose fascination with people who are down on their luck. Shows like *Intervention* or any of the plethora of prison documentaries dotting the landscape of television probably wouldn't have had such a successful run if we as people didn't take a small pleasure in seeing those who are worse off than we are. It is sort a smug little triumph to sip your wine while watching the fall down drunk on TV get arrested or dragged to detox. We can enjoy our jammy Cabernet and feel superior because we can drink without it ruining our lives. As a people, we like to feel that no matter how bad off we are, there is someone somewhere who is worse off. The parking ticket you got today feels a lot less heavy when you can watch a guy serving life for murder bare his soul to a camera crew through bullet proof glass.

These shows fill a strange, deep void in us. With the push of a button we can be privy to people's deaths, crimes, shortcomings, embarrassments, and sob-stories and switch away when the content gets too real or something better comes on. I am as guilty as the next person of partaking in this technological voyeurism. I will often loose myself in hours of prison shows, only to switch the TV off and remember that I am actually going to be there the following morning.

Watch all the real-life prison shows you want, but it won't capture even an iota of the horror and monotony that is a prisoner's life. For legal reasons there are no shows profiling locked up kids, which is a shame for the heartbreak junkies. There is nothing more dismal than hearing a fourteen-year-old girl recount how she looked for the Big Dipper outside of her cell window last night or having a sixteen-year-old father show you the battered photo of his daughter that he keeps in his sock.

Yes, these kids made choices, no one is disputing that. However, the nature of the penalty and the spirit in which it was issued must be assessed. Are we giving a teenager a two-year sentence behind bars for stealing someone's car because we think that they will be magically rehabilitated? Or have we become a vigilante society, treating criminal kids like scores we have to settle?

Nothing gets fixed behind bars. All that happens is that kids spend time with other, more hardened criminals. They get to reconnect with homies and drug dealers from their neighborhoods, they get jailhouse tattoos that are as good as street cred, they get a little shrewder, a bit harder. They establish a record, get out on probation which is set up to fail, violate something like a curfew clause and end up back behind bars within a month or so.

A student just came back into juvenile hall because she had a cell phone on her. That was it. Part of her probation contract stated that she could not have a cell phone on her. Never mind that her mother was in labor and wanted to be able to call her daughter when her little brother was born. Now she will be locked up for the first month of her little brother's life because a turned-off cell phone was found in her backpack during a classroom search at the continuation school she had just transitioned to. Did she do something wrong? Technically, yes. But did she deserve to be locked up for a month for it?

A boy's probation officer asked if he had change for a twenty-dollar bill. He pulled out the one hundred dollars in tens that his mom had given him to buy new shoes with. His probation officer assumed that he was selling drugs and booked him into the hall for two months. His mom protested that she had not only given her son the money, but that she had worked overtime at her two jobs to save the money to do so. He lost two months of his life because of an assumption.

Before I took this job, I was considering going into probation work. I am glad I did not. While I have the upmost respect for good probation officers, the vast majority have way too many kids on their docket and the only way for them to check up on their kids is through a twice monthly phone call to kids on house arrest or a drug-screening urine test. A missed day at school or a dirty pee test often means that the kid will be locked up for a few weeks. So somewhere between the violation and being locked up and then released two weeks later, the kid is supposed to somehow fix whatever is causing them to use drugs or get into trouble.

As a society we cannot continue to expect kids to magically fix themselves, incarcerated or not. If a kid on the outs was in some sort of trouble, the average parent would try to find the source of the issue and remedy it. Would counseling help? Perhaps a tutor for an academic issue? Telling a kid to fix themselves and then walking away before we have taught them how doesn't just reek of laziness; it screams of a societal apathy that we should be ashamed of.

Kids don't just suddenly develop healthy, functional tools and coping mechanisms. These things need to be taught to them and they need to be taught by a safe, reliable adult. Most of my students are missing some or all of the tools that a teenager needs to navigate through adolescence. Either through neglect, abuse, poverty, or bad choices, these kids have made it to adolescence lacking some vital strategies to deal with bad feelings or unfortunate events. So they have found coping mechanisms to compensate. No healthy family unit? Join a gang. Battling depression or trying to deal with a trauma? Start doing drugs or cutting. When healthy tools are not taught to kids, they will do what they have to do to deal with uncomfortable feelings and trauma.

When a fourteen-year-old is on their ninth time in juvenile hall in two years, something is not working at the judicial level. When students come into class at age seventeen unable to identify a noun or spell 'school', something is not working at the educational level. When kids talk about how they are going to reoffend right before Christmas to make sure they are locked up and that they will actually get a meal and a present this year, something is not working at the family level.

I place a lot of blame on parents. This is your kid, not the government's or the school's. This isn't to say that the government and the school system do not play a roll in the upbringing, but the vast majority of parenting needs to fall on the parents. You made the choice to have sex and with that comes the risk of having a baby. I know a lot of people will disagree with me on this, and I am not trying to say that a lot of parents don't need and deserve help, but the burden of parenting falls on the shoulders of those who produced the child in question. Sadly, some parents choose to checkout, either emotionally or physically, leaving a gapping hole in their children, one that will often be filled with bad habits and destructive tendencies.

One student in particular comes to mind. Eduardo is so quiet that one would think he was mute. He averages a few sentences a week. The boy will go for days without uttering a word, communicating in grunts and shakes of the head. Yet because he is quiet, no one seems to think that his behavior is indicative of an emotional issue. Often teachers focus on the loud ones, the rambunctious and the hyperactive. The ones that are quiet and virtually invisible often get overlooked. A lot of teachers see them as ideal students because they never speak. But being almost completely non-verbal is not normal for a teenager. The quiet ones are the ones that concern me the most.

I had referred Eduardo for a special education evaluation, hoping that he could get some services, and Wendy had been working overtime to assess him. Even she was skeptical that there was an issue at first, telling Nikki that the issue was probably just me and my lack of teaching experience. Thankfully after she met with him, she quickly realized how much pain Eduardo was in and how desperately he needed help. After weeks of tying up the loose ends of all of his paperwork, Wendy announced that once the IEP meeting could be held with Eduardo's mother, the boy could begin to officially receive weekly mental health services such as counseling and possibly medication, as well as official placement into the special education classroom for the subjects he struggled the most in. Since Eduardo was a minor, he could not legally be given these resources without the consent of his custodial parent. Easier said than done. Wendy left fourteen messages on the mother's cell phone and work answering machine, begging her to call back for the sake of her son's well-being. The mother never returned a single phone call.

"And since she won't return my phone calls, I can't sign him up for services. I literally have to file everything we have done and put it away." She closes the thick manila folder before her, a sigh of defeating leaking out between her words.

"You mean he won't get his services because his mother is too lazy or self-centered to return a phone call about her son?"

"Pretty much. Legally, my hands are tied. If she won't sign the paper, the kid is going to fall through yet another crack. He is an emotionally disturbed kid who is going to keep being pushed through the system because his mom won't return a phone call. It breaks my heart."

The school and the mental health department were offering this boy all of the services, both emotionally and academically, that he needed. And his mother would not sign the one piece of paper that would give her son these things. This is an example of the family sabotaging the child, which is sadly not an isolated or even unique experience.

And I see red when I hear the whole 'pull yourself up by you bootstraps' blather. Of course there are those who can turn their lives around, apropos of nothing, but it's rare enough at an adult level, and even scarcer among children. Humans gravitate towards what is comfortable, safe, and easy. It takes a mature person to do what is foreign and difficult because they either don't like the choices they have been making or they want something new and better for themselves. If a teenager's coping mechanisms have been violence and substance abuse, it is unlikely that one day they will wake up and decide to start forming healthy emotional and mental tools for dealing with life. Kids need help. It should not take a child being arrested or shot or kicked out of school for a parent, teacher, relative, neighbor or someone to realize something is wrong.

A dysfunctional level of society, whether educational or familial or judicial, should be noticed by another facet. If something is dysfunctional at home, the school or social services should notice. If education is not working, then the government or the family should speak up. There has to be an accountability between all the societal components. Otherwise we end up with what we have; a series of government-funded slices of Swiss cheese posing as safety nets to catch the kids as they fall through. Inevitably they hit the rock bottom floor of juvenile hall, which provides security in incarceration. It is the one floor that won't give way beneath them.

March 16

"Happy Women's History Month!" I may as well have greeted the boys in Swahili. "The month of women! A month of honoring women who have made pioneering achievements in various fields and changed the world in some way. How do you guys not know about this?"

"Like the field of cooking?" Jesus asks, his brows knit in confusion

"Oh shit, she's getting the crazy eye! Say you're sorry!" Juan hisses at Jesus.

"I am going to pretend you didn't say that. Today we are going to study the role of the protagonist and the antagonist in the narrative." I was suddenly before an entire class of deer in headlights.

"Does anyone know what a protagonist is?" Crickets. "An antagonist? A narrative?"

"Isn't that a person who lives in teepees?" Kevin asks.

"Let me back up here. A narrative is just a fancy, more academic word for a story. A story has lots of parts in it. You can't just say Bob woke up and then he went to sleep and that's the end. That's not a story."

"Well, not a very good one," Jose concedes.

"Exactly. Things have to happen in a story. There has to be a setting, the where and when, and there has to be a series of events and there has to be characters in books, movies, and songs. Narratives can be literary or musical or cinematic."

"Cinematic?" Juan rolls the word around his mouth like a jawbreaker.

"Having to do with cinema. The movies. Characters are a really important part of a story. If a story didn't have characters in it, it would just be someone talking about a place. Pretty boring."

"So you need people?" Juan asks.

"In books and in life, too. People make a story interesting and they make life interesting, too. If you have ever seen a Disney movie, you know that characters can be animals or even inanimate objects, like in *Beauty and the Beast.*"

"So what were those words you used before? Pro-something?" Jose asks.

"Protagonist and antagonist. Anyone want to guess what those words mean?"

"Well if you are anti-something, it means you are against it. So is the antagonist the bad guy?"

"Usually, yes. And usually the protagonist is the good guy. But the actual meaning of protagonist is the main character. So they can be bad sometimes. And if the guy trying to stop him is a good guy, then he is..."

"The antagonist!" Jesus crows triumphantly.

"So we are the antagonists? I mean in life, right?" Carlos asks.

"Maybe you are," Jorge growls.

"He's right. If the law is right, and we break it, that makes us wrong. That makes us bad to cops and society," Jose says.

"Can something be right for some people and wrong for others?" Kevin asks.

"I think we all have our own ideas. If my kids are starving, and I steal some food for them, then I did the right thing for my family but to the law, it's wrong." Jose speaks slowly, measuring the weight of each word.

"Exactly! And characters in stories whose actions are seen by some as noble and seen by others as being villainous are usually pretty interesting. Look at Robin Hood."

"I never met him. He in here?" Juan's hackles are going up as they always do when a new person is brought to his attention. Every person is yet another thing to be assessed and put into the friend or enemy category. Life for a gang member must be exhausting. To have to analyze every new person you meet within seconds, to miss out on the joy of discovering a new human because you are not sure whether or not he wants to kill you.

"*Robin Hood*. The story. You know about *Robin Hood*?" The deer have returned to the classroom. "Raise your hand if you know who Robin Hood is."

A single hand goes up.

"Marco, what do you know about Robin Hood?"

"He lived in a forest a long time ago. And he would steal

169

from the rich and give to the poor." A glimmer of something shoots through his eyes. It's too fleeting to process, but it looks dangerously close to being pride.

"This real?" Kevin asks.

"He is a character in a very old story about a guy who was the best archer and swordsman. Over time the story changed and he became a guy who would steal from wealthy, corrupt men and give to the poor people of England."

"He's bad-ass!" Juan crows. "Why don't we read about him?"

"He is one of the most famous characters in literature. There have been books and cartoons and movies made about him."

"What's so big about him stealing? I steal and ain't nobody writing books about me," Jorge snarls.

"Well, I guess it's not just that he stole. A lot of people steal. It was his motivation that people respected. Characters who go against a corrupt, powerful force are characters that we like to know about."

"Are we going to learn about him?" Juan asks.

"I hadn't planned on it. I hadn't even planned on really talking about him at all. Aside from using him as an example. But now that you bring it up, he is a great example of how the protagonist and the antagonist can be a blurry distinction."

"They stink?"

"No, distinction means a difference. Sometimes who is right and who is wrong is not totally clear."

"I want to know more about Robin Hood, Miss Wehr," Juan says.

At lunch, I tried to figure out how I could do this. We have a fairly rigorous curriculum schedule to follow. The books we had to teach were already plotted out for the year and inserting another one, let alone coming up with the money to buy a classroom set, seemed impossible. How could I show the boys the story of *Robin Hood* without it taking a month or so out of our curriculum trajectory?

March 22

"We get to watch a movie?" Jose is incredulous. "Is it a new movie? Does it have hot chicks in it?"

"Yes, you get to watch a movie. No, it's an old movie. And stop calling women chicks. They are not baby chickens."

"Sorry. Does it have attractive females in it?"

"So what movie is it?" Juan is looking at me warily.

I hold up my battered copy of the 1938 version of *Robin Hood*.

"That looks hella old," Carlos groans.

"Why you always complaining, man? We never get to watch movies in here and now she isn't gonna let us do it again if you don't shut up," Jose growls.

Carlos put up his hands in defeat and leans silently back into his seat.

"A film is a visual narrative. It's a story that we get to watch. And we can interact with a visual narrative the same way we can with a written text."

"What does that mean? Are we going to have to answer questions or something?"

Grinning, I hold up a list of questions that I had typed up while watching the movie last night. The cacophony of groans that rose from the classroom was enough to make Mr. Robbins pull his sunglasses down to the tip of his nose, assess what was going on, and chuckle.

"Every movie asks a question and then it answers itself in its unfolding. The question here is was Robin Hood a protagonist because of his intentions or an antagonist because of his actions?"

"I take it back. I don't want to know about Robin Hood," Jose says.

"We have to answer all of these?" Carlos has a look on his face that I haven't seen since my ex-boyfriend found a Band-Aid in his burrito.

"No, Carlos. I thought maybe you could just answer whichever ones seem really easy."

I slide the DVD in and press play. And magic happens. The boys are enthralled at a level I have never seen. They cheer when he wins a sword fight and boo when he is arrested. They cluck their tongues in disapproval at the treatment of the peasants and laugh at the bumbling of Friar Tuck. They whistle their approval at the kissing at the window scene and are confused when Robin Hood left without pushing the issue further.

"That's it?" Jose hisses, leaning over to me. "That's all he's going to do? Just kiss her?"

I lean over my desk, whispering back, "Back then, that's about all you could do before you were married. Anything else would ruin her reputation and make him seem like a pushy jerk."

"Man, things have changed." Jose sits back up, shaking his head.

The watching and the question answering took two class periods. At the end of the second day, I asked them what their thoughts were.

"Robin Hood was cool. He tried to help out the poor people. So he was a good guy. Sorry...a...what is it? A protagonist, " Juan says.

"And the law was the antagonist," Jose adds. "Isn't that kinda backwards? The law is usually right and the bad guy is usually...well, bad."

"That's a good point and possibly part of the reason why Robin Hood is such an enduring and endearing character. We cheer for him because he is the little guy going against the big, bad government."

"Don't see why homie had to wear those tights, though, " Jorge grumbles.

"Haha! Can you imagine if we showed up to rob someone wearing tights? They would laugh at us!" Marco chuckles.

"So, having seen this, can you better understand why Robin Hood could be viewed as both an antagonist and a protagonist?" I ask.

"Yea. It's like all about your point of view, right? So if I am a cop and I look at him, it's bad. But if I am a poor person and he has just given me food for my family, it's good." Jose says. "Can we watch another old movie tomorrow?"

Driving home that afternoon, I mull over the fact that save one, none of my kids knew anything about Robin Hood. They knew literally nothing about him. I could have told them he was a narcoleptic giraffe and they would have believed me. The vast majority of my students were not read to as children. As a result, they not only have low reading comprehension, deficient attention spans, poor vocabulary, but also a total lack of knowledge about stories that we assume every kid would know by the time they reach sixteen. *The Cat in the Hat* and *Little Red Riding Hood* are all as foreign to most of my kids as astrophysics or Norse mythology. It was just never a part of their childhood. Ask most kindergartners today to tell you the story of *Three Little Pigs* and they will be able to rattle off some variation on the classic tale. Ask an incarcerated teenager and chances are they will have only a vague recollection of fairy tales or have no knowledge of it whatsoever. The literary building blocks that we assume all children ascended on their way to school were simply not present for my students.

"I'm back!" Like a triumphant Viking returning from battle, Antonio is all smiles and fireworks. Half of his face is covered in road rash. He has been in and out of here over a dozen times in the past two years. If we had a punch card like a frozen yogurt shop, he would definitely be getting a free swirl right about now.

There are no other students in the class at the moment, so I have a chance to speak candidly with him. "Antonio, why do you keep coming here? Why do you feel the need to steal all the time?"

"I am good at it. And you enjoy what you are good at." This is a new, fresh hardness. Something else has happened that he is not telling me. "I have to do me, you feel me?"

He was starting to get on the defensive. 'I have to do me' is a cockeyed cop-out the kids use a lot, roughly translating to 'I do what I want because it pleases me'.

"Yea but when you do you, you disrespect others. For someone who values respect so much that he has it tattooed on his arm, you sure don't practice what you preach."

Antonio's right eye twitches for a moment. A few of the girls here belong to the stable of underage prostitutes that he and his cousin oversee. He runs this operation in conjunction with a lucrative stolen electronics ring.

"I don't mean no disrespect, but you don't know what it's like to not have what you need. I need money. And I gotta do what I gotta do to take care of myself and my family."

"I understand that you want to help your family and that is honorable. But taking from others is not the way to do it."

"You sound like my PO." He rolls his eyes and leans back into his seat, arms folded. He is trying to pull up the rope ladder. Thankfully, I am an excellent climber.

"No. I care about your future, not your past. But most of all, I care about you. And I am telling you this from love, there is no honor among thieves. Deep down you know what you are doing is wrong, but I understand that what you want can be stronger than what is right."

Antonio is silent but his rapid blinking showed me that he was listening. I had less than a minute before the other students showed up and I have to talk fast. His pursed lips quivered for a moment, but he held fast to his silence.

"Everyone struggles with wanting something they can't have. You are not the only one who wants something. But the earmark of maturity is waiting. Acquiring something the right way, as opposed to the quick way. You don't think I would love to have nice clothes and a new car? Hell, yes. But I am not about to risk my freedom because I want something. And what about girls you run? You are breaking their families when you exploit their daughters like that, not to mention how much you are hurting them."

"They come to me. I just show them that they can make money on something they are already giving away for free. Think of me as an entrepreneur. I teach them how to make profit on a built-in product."

"Yea right, an entrepreneur. You are the first person in the history of the world to pimp teenage girls. And they are people! They are not product!"

To this, he made a fist with his left hand, displaying the letters MOB tattooed on his knuckles. "Money Over Bitches. That's my motto. And I do what I gotta do to get mine."

"Antonio, what happened to you? When are you going to actually see this for what it is? Are you just going to keep on with this until they have to carry you out in a fucking body bag?"

Antonio flinches like I just struck him. The boys began to file into class, calling out their greetings to Antonio. He is far away and I can't reach him.

A frustrating conversation, but it will not detract from the fact that today was an especially exciting day. We had just received our first letter from Darwin, the child in Bolivia that our class was sponsoring. The letter was written in Spanish. Also included was a picture that he drew of his school, a small orange building with one tree out front.

"He wrote us a letter?" Kevin is wide-eyed. "What does he say? Can we read it?"

"I don't read Spanish. Can any of you guys translate this?"

Juan takes the letter from my hands. "It says, 'Hello. My name is Darwin. I am nine years old. I live in Bolivia. I go to school and I like to play soccer and play with my brothers and sisters. I have seven sisters!' Holy shit! This kid has a big family! 'I want to be a doctor when I grow up. Thank you for sponsoring me'." Juan looks at the letter in his hands like it's a relic from an ancient civilization, a fossil of hope and innocence. "Bolivia. Where is that?"

"It's in Europe, right?" Carlos asks.

"Nah, homie. It's in South America," Jose corrects him.

"It's a beautiful country, but is considered repressed economically which means the government is not doing the best job taking care of its people. Some people don't have jobs and some people live in poverty. It's the third largest producer of cocaine. There is also a lot of child labor. Kids as young as Darwin sometimes have to work very dangerous jobs to support their families. You guys can only imagine the difficulties that this boy must live with, growing up among poverty and drugs. Some of you may know all too well what this is like."

"What's poverty?" Antonio asks. "I heard that word a lot before but I never knew what it meant."

"Does anyone know what that word means?" Every boy shakes his head no. I have to think how to phrase this delicately enough to not sound accusatory. "Poverty is sort of a state of being in which someone is very poor. Like someone who lives in poverty might not have enough money for food and rent or be without a house or may rely on government assistance to make ends meet."

"Wow. So that means I live in poverty, " muses Jorge.

"Don't stress, man. I think most of us live in poverty, " Juan mutters.

"And that's something you may have in common with Darwin. His family struggles to keep everyone fed and clothed and keep a roof overhead. Your family may also struggle with someone of those things. Hardship is everywhere, sadly. That may be something to consider when we write letters to Darwin."

"What kind of things should we write to him about?" Carlos asks.

"I don't see what the big deal is," groans Jorge from the corner of the room, slouched low in his desk. "I come from a broke-ass home, too. Ain't nobody ever helped me out or wrote me letters."

"We all come from a broke-ass home, but maybe we can make this kid feel happy. There's nothing wrong with that. So it says here that this kid lives in a house with dirt floors and he only gets one pair of shoes a year." Juan points to the information sheet the organization had given us.

The kids murmur their amazement, shaking their heads at this level of poverty. Some of them seemed to be realizing that while they may not have an iPod or a nice car, their circumstances were not nearly as dire as a child in a small village in the heart of South America. This was exactly what I wanted, to open at least a few of their eyes to the plight of people that didn't live in the three block radius of their neighborhood.

Marco is crying. Tears are rolling down his cheeks as he stares at his desk, trying not to show his face to the boys seated next to him. I motion for Mr. Robbins to keep an eye on the kids and I pull Marco out of the classroom.

In the cool hush of the hallway, Marco begins to sob. "That little boy, living in dirt with no shoes. I know about that. My cousins live on the streets in Mexico. They have no home. They sleep outside every night and sometimes they don't eat for a few days. When I go see them, I give them all my clothes that don't fit me and my dad will buy them food. I worry that someone will hurt them because they don't have a home."

"I know it's sad, sweetie, but we are going to make something better for a kid somewhere and that's what we should focus on. I love that you feel compassion for Darwin and that you don't like the idea of a kid not having a home. That shows that you have a good heart."

"People think that just because we are criminals, we don't have feelings." He takes a deep breath, squares his shoulders, and walks back into class. This will be the first time that the boys see one of their own openly weeping in class.

Please let them be compassionate. I don't know who I am asking this of, but I hope they are listening.

"Hey, little homie. I cry too sometimes. A real man can cry. Ain't no shame in it," Juan murmurs to him. He reaches out and squeezes Marco's shoulder. Marco looks up at him, bleary-eyed and grateful.

April 4

Whether by chronic truancy or family issues, stints in rehab or deportation, there are massive missing chunks in my student's educational foundation. Extending to all areas of study, my fellow teachers can often be overheard lamenting a student's inability to divide or find Sweden on a map. This is not to say our students are not intelligent; they are some of the most perceptive and gifted human beings I have ever known. It's just that when the things that a teacher assumes a student can do by a certain age are not in place, it makes bringing the kid up to grade level a hell of a lot harder.

Frustrated with Eduardo's consistently illegible handwriting, I drop myself into a desk beside him, shoving a paper at him. "Eduardo, we have to talk about this."

Eduardo winces at how quickly I have sat down in his broad bubble and how abrupt my tone is. He is so emaciated and pale, the bags under his eyes so hollow and bruise-colored, that the other kids have taken to calling him Skeletor. "My handwriting?"

"I have tried and tried but I cannot read this paper. It's like some cuneiform-hieroglyphic language." This is not exaggerating; it looks like it was written by a dyslexic chicken.

"I never learned how to write," he whispers.

I raise my eyebrows at this. I have had students say they could not read, could not write, and Jesus even said he was allergic to pencils during our first week of school. Sometimes they are telling the truth, albeit an exaggerated version of it and sometimes they are just straight up lying. "What do you mean you never learned how to write? Your teachers never taught you the alphabet? I find that hard to believe. You read very well and you write a lot. It's just that what you are writing is really hard to decode."

"I learned my letters, but I can't make them look how they are supposed to look." Eduardo is struggling with how close I am to him, this dialogue causing beads of sweat to dot his upper lip. "I was born in Mexico and my first couple years of school, I was just taught by my uncles on the ranch we lived on. When we moved up to California, I went to regular school for a few years, but I couldn't speak English very well and it was really hard to keep up. Plus I missed a lot of school. Mom was in and out of prison and when she was out, we were always on the run or living in hotels or cars. She was high all the time so she couldn't help me with my homework. It got so overwhelming that I fell behind in school and just stopped going."

"When was this?"

"Fifth grade."

"Didn't your school notice you were gone?"

"I don't know. They may have not been able to get ahold of us. Our address and phone number changed a lot. Sometimes we didn't have one or the other. Maybe they just figured I was a Mexican kid with a druggie mom so they kind of expected it."

"You don't read at a fifth grade level and you can write more than someone at that grade level, even if the letters don't look right. Please don't think this means that you are not intelligent or a good student. This is just something we will work on together. "

"Can you print me out the alphabet? The whole thing? I don't know all my letters. Maybe I can practice them during our program time on the unit." He is speaking to his knees, rocking in his seat. This is so wildly out of his comfort zone, this asking for and needing something from another person.

"You don't know the whole alphabet? Your uncle in Mexico didn't teach you all of the letters?"

"My uncle was a Sureno. He only taught me the letters M and S. I learned some of the others from watching kid's shows in Mexico. I wanted to know all of them, but one day I learned the letter N. When I told my uncle, he kicked me in the stomach." He swallows this memory, a hand rubbing his concave abdomen. "When my uncle found out I became a Northerner, he said I was no longer a member of the family."

"No one here will ever hurt you for wanting to learn. And even though someone did once, I am glad you still want to. I will let you borrow a penmanship book, too."

"You will give it to me?" His head flies up like a snapped guitar string. "You would trust me with one of your books?"

"Why wouldn't I trust you? You have never lied to me before. Plus I know exactly where you live for the next few months."

"Nobody ever trusted me with anything before." He furrows his brows at me, lips pursed like he is whistling silently. "Thank you."

"For trusting you?"

He shakes his head. "No, for making me feel like I deserve to be trusted."

April 12

"How is this going to help me in the world?" Jose looks up from his adverb and adjective worksheet. "How is knowing this stuff going to help me get a job and make money and be happy and all that? How does this help?"

"You need to know the parts of speech. That's one of the standards that the Department of Education feels is important. Looking at a word and knowing if it's a noun or an adverb or a preposition or whatever."

"I get that. But how does it help me?" Jose is getting frustrated. He does not feel like he is being heard. And I guess I really am not hearing him. "I mean in a job interview, nobody is going to ask me what an adjective is, are they?"

"Honestly, no. I highly doubt that knowing that the word 'richly' is an adverb is going to help you a great deal."

"So why are we doing this, Miss Wehr?" Antonio asks. At this point, the whole class had ceased working and is observing our discussion.

"Ideally, you would all finish high school and go onto college. And to get through things like all of the tests in high school, you need to know the fundamentals of grammar."

"Miss Wehr, I don't want to disrespect what you are trying to do here. I appreciate it and all, but not many of us going to college," Jose smiles sadly.

"I hope that none of you feel that college is off-limits. You all possess what it takes. But college or not, you will all have to make an honest living one day."

A ripple of snickers ran through the classroom.

"An honest living? How the hell am I going to make an honest living?"

"By getting a job like any one else, Carlos."

"Who is going to hire a seventeen year old kid from the projects who is covered in tattoos and has felonies on his record? Working a legit job, working honest just isn't an option for us. We kind of have to take to the streets to survive. The regular world does not want us."

I want to argue with him, but I realize it would be a lie. It is easier and more profitable for my students to make a living selling drugs on the streets. Honest work means more work for less money. "How many of you guys think that a regular nine-to-five job is off limits to you?"

Every hand in the room goes up. My breath leaves me in one fell swoop. This is a steep incline I have to ascend. "Give me reasons why."

"Carlos covered most of them. I mean between our tattoos, our records, and our lack of education, we are kind of shit out of luck," Kevin adds.

"Let me put it like this," continues Jose. "I come into an interview with you. I have visible tattoos that are obviously gang-related. I have an attempted murder and multiple drug felonies on my record. I have a strike. I don't own a suit. I have no references that a boss would think are good. I have no work experience because I have been in and out of the hall since I was thirteen. The few jobs I had were all under-the-table construction or landscaping and those were both with my uncle. I can't use him as a reference because he got deported last year and no one has heard from him since. I don't even have a fucking address to put down because I have been homeless for the past six months."

Hearing all of the obstacles my kids face when trying to find a job lined up like that is overwhelming. If I faced even half of those challenges, I would be too discouraged to even attempt a job interview. And for a brief moment, I catch a glimpse of the despair and hopelessness that faces my students whenever they think of their future.

"What can I teach you in the classroom that will make at least trying to get a job a little easier?"

"What to say in an interview," Jose says. "And what NOT to say in an interview."

"How to act and talk proper. And how to balance your money. My mom always talks about balancing a checkbook and I have no idea what the hell she is talking about," Antonio adds.

"Balancing a checkbook is just about making sure that your income doesn't exceed your expenses." It strikes me that I have absolutely no idea how much money is in my checking account at the moment.

"For an English teacher, you sure don't talk clear," Carlos frowns at me.

"Let me explain this differently. Imagine if Antonio had 75 bananas..."

"What's up now, bitches? 75 bananas!" Antonio spins around in his seat, grinning at the other boys with his fists above his head.

"You're stupid, spending all your money on bananas," Jorge shakes his head at Antonio's wasteful behavior.

"Yea, but you know what? We run outta bananas, guess who's going to be your best friend? That's right! Antonio the banana king!"

"Maybe we should tackle financial planning another time. So what do you guys know for sure that you should not do during an interview?" I don't even know why I bother with lesson plans. Half the time we end up doing something else.

"Don't show up high!"

"Wear pants!"

"Don't hit on the person interviewing you. I did that. Didn't get the job, " Antonio grins.

"These are rather obvious things to avoid in an interview, but there are also more subtle mistakes that a lot of people make in an interview. Let's look at posture, to start." My students are slouched down in their desks with legs splayed open. This is their usual position in class. The boys look at each other, realize what I am getting at, and hurriedly straighten themselves. "Good, that's a start. It's not a good idea to look comatose or drunk during an interview."

"Do people actually care how you sit?" asks Jose.

"It's not something you will be asked about on your resume but your body language speaks volumes. If I was interviewing someone and they were slouched down in the seat, with their feet up on the furniture, that would tell me that this person does not care about how other people view him. That would reflect poorly on my company if I hired him, so I would be inclined to hire someone who showed me respect through how they sat and acted."

The boys nod knowingly, a few quickly removing their feet from the desks in front of them as I drag two chairs to the front of the room. "We are going to do job interviews for the rest of class. I am going to ask you the questions that an employer would ask you and I want you to answer them as honestly as possible. Then we will talk about what was done right and what we can work on."

The boys laughingly chide Juan as he saunters up, dragging his feet in a nonchalant manner as he approaches the chair. He falls into it with so much force that the chair scoots back a few inches.

"Okay, we already have an issue. Can anyone tell me what was wrong about how Juan approached me?"

"He didn't shake your hand. I heard you should always shake a boss's hand, " Jose says.

"What about how he walked up?"

"Less swagger."

"Right. I don't think you should Crip walk into an interview. Sends a bad message."

"Okay, I will walk more like a white person. Can we keep going?" Juan sighs.

"So Juan, why do you want this job?"

"I need money. I have a lot of court fees to pay."

"Don't mention your legal shit!" Antonio calls out. "And sit up, man!"

"I want this job because I like working and I...I..." Juan is floundering.

"Because you like my business and you think you will be a great member of our team." I prompt.

"Because I like your business and I will be a great member of the team." Juan echoes, his eyes falling to the floor. Before I could ask the next question, he lets out a yelp and jumps onto his chair. "Spider!"

The other boys follow suit, screeching and climbing onto their desks, with shouts of, "Kill it! Kill it!"

A small black bug is waddling past my desk. "Can someone grab that and put it outside?" I ask, looking around the room. Of the nine young men in my class, all of whom spend almost every waking minute trying to prove how tough they are, not one wanted to touch the bug.

"I ain't touching that thing. It's going to bite me!" yells Kevin, tucking his feet up under him.

"Most of you have either been shot or stabbed at some point but you are scared to touch a bug?"

"Miss Wehr, I will take care of it," Eduardo says softly.

Stoically, he walks the bug to the door and gently sets it down outside. The other boys watch him with reverence and respectful quiet. As he returns to his desk, an unmistakable smile of triumph on his face, the other boys clap him on the back and whistle their approval.

Bringing the class back to the lesson takes a few minutes, especially since they are now convinced that the classroom is full of bugs and start throwing erasers at one another while screaming, "BUG!" Sometimes I feel like a second grade teacher. Juan returns to his hot seat in the front of the class and we pick up where we left off.

"So what do you think you would bring to my company?"

"Huh?"

"Don't say 'huh'!" Marco yells from the back of the room.

"Oh shit, sorry. I mean, excuse me."

"I will rephrase the question. Why do you think your presence will make my company better?"

"Presents? I have to give you presents?" He looks like someone who just realized he showed up to a black tie event in jeans.

The interest they are showing in their futures is heart-warming. This is really all I can do: get them to think in terms of what comes next. So many of my students do not expect to live past eighteen, that the idea of planning for a future just seems idiotic. I want them so badly to realize that their life is their own choice, that they can live a long and happy life, if only they chose to.

April 15

The Bard and the boys ware becoming fast friends. Once we had gotten over the initial rough patch with *Romeo and Juliet*, the kids had fallen in love with Shakespeare. I think they were sort of proud to be given such a challenging text. They carried their books with the titles facing out, halfheartedly complaining about having to read Shakespeare to any staff that would listen. When we began *Julius Caesar* a week ago, the boys had been eager and much more open-minded. They had conquered him before so he was much less daunting the second go-around.

"Every story asks a question and then answers itself. Having read *Romeo and Juliet*, what question do you think that book was asking?"

"I think it was asking how far would you go for love? Like would you go against your family and your friends? Would you be with a sworn enemy if you were in love with them?" Jorge says.

"Would you?" Juan turns back to Jorge.

"Would I date a scrap? Hell, nah. Might as well date a dog." Jorge folds his arms over his chest. There is some new pink, puffy scar tissue on his arm in the shape of a giant 'N'. Someone has been doing some carving in his free time. "Would you?"

"I did! I mean she wasn't really with it hardcore. Her family was into that shit. Man, they didn't like me coming around. Her brother put a gun in my face the first night I went to pick her up for a date."

"How the hell was there a second date?"

"Man, you didn't see this girl. She was hella fine. Like Selena Gomez and Megan Fox all smushed together." Juan smashes the clay of his perfect woman between his hands, eyes glowing like a Lite-Brite under covers.

"Yea, I would take a gun to the face for a chick like that, too, " Marco chuckles.

"It don't matter how hot she is; you are walking a dangerous line," Jorge snarls. He waits for a second for someone to agree with him and looks a bit startled by the silence. "What if her family caught you slipping and smoked you? You really want to die for some pussy?"

"Jorge, watch your mouth." My patience with him is fraying daily.

"Sorry. You really want to die for some labia?" They must be studying the reproductive system in science class.

"I guess I didn't think about it. I just wanted to be with her. She was amazing. But her brothers said that if she kept dating me, they would kill me. So she dumped with me. Last I heard she was dating a Southerner. He got her pregnant and broke her jaw." Juan's voice floats away like smoke.

"I think the book is asking if we can control who we love," Antonio says.

"I don't think we can. I think we just love who we love and that's it. Love is bigger than people and situations," Marco says. "I can't ever stop loving my family or my homies. That's not something I have control over."

"But with women, you can control that. You can make yourself not love a woman if you have to," Jorge snarls, still glaring at Juan. "If I fell in love with a girl and I found out that her family were scraps...sorry, Southerners, I would make myself not love her. I ain't trying to be no *Romeo and Juliet*."

"So what's the question that Shakespeare is asking in *Julius Caesar*?" Jose asks.

"I think he is talking about choices. About decisions and how those change our lives," Antonio says. "Brutus and Cassius have to make a choice. They have to decide whether or not to kill Caesar. They have to chose between their friend and their city. If they let their friend live, they think the city that they love will fall apart. And if they kill him, they think the city will be better, but they will have to live with the guilt." Antonio is speaking from some dark, deep part of himself. He traces the corners of his book, staring at it like it he is seeing his face in a mirror for the first time.

"Hell of a choice to have to make. How do you chose between someone who is like your brother and your home? I couldn't make a choice like that," Juan says, sounding smaller than I have ever heard him. His voice is an aftershock of itself.

"It's not that hard. You gave your word to be down for your hood. That's the bottom line. If someone gets in the way, you have to handle it. It's not difficult." Jorge's words send a sick, cold shock down my back. How can he possibly believe this? How can anyone?

"So buildings and streets are more important than people?" I have to choose my words very carefully here. One misstep and this conversation will shatter.

"It's not just the parts of a city. It's what it represents. It's your home. It's what you have to protect. You made that promise. And sometimes you have to go against someone if they are not honoring the commitment they made."

"So loyalty to a city is more important than loyalty to a person?"

"It's not that simple, Miss Wehr. I don't know how to make you get it. When you are part of something, it's part of you. It's not something you just abandon, even if everyone says it's bad. That's why Brutus felt so guilty and unsure about what he was doing, killing Caesar and everything. He couldn't remove that part of himself, that love of his city. And in the end it was bigger and more powerful than his love for his best friend."

For the first time, the boys seem very much alone in this room. Every one of them seems somehow removed from the others, thinly outlined in an isolation that only comes with the knowledge that your deepest connections are not so very deep at all. That every person you love will always love something else more than you. Their loyalty to one another is actually quite brittle and fleeting, regardless of how many times they get it tattooed onto them. They are not connected in any way, they do not touch. They are hundreds and thousands of boys and young men who are alone in a churning mob.

"We are all Brutus, in some way," Juan murmurs softly. "We feel pulled in so many directions. Between our family and our homies and what's right and wrong and everything. We are supposed to be loyal to everything and we have to make a choice."

"You know, I always thought that I would never read anything by Shakespeare. I thought I wouldn't like it or it would just be confusing. But I get it and I actually like it. It's like even back then, people were going through the same shit we are today. We are all the same people, just trying to go through life and make the best decisions but we mess up a lot and we make mistakes,"

Antonio says. "We all have the same worries and problems. In Ancient Rome, they were worried about their city and fighting with their friends and having to stand up for what they believe in. We aren't so different from these guys. I can't believe I am saying this, but I would actually tell people to read this book."

"I don't know, this isn't the easiest stuff to understand sometimes," Marco shakes his head warily.

"You just have to explain it to them in a way they would understand," Antonio says. "Like you tell them there is this homie Cassius and he is a shot caller. And there is a another homie named Brutus and he is a little hitta'. Cassius green-lighted Casear because he can't run shit."

"You left out the part where he shanks Caesar!" Jose says. "But I don't get what he meant when he said *et tu Brutus.*"

"*Et tu Brutus* just means you are hella shady, homie," Antonio explains.

"How the hell are you gonna make a homie read this shit?" Jorge sneers, shaking his book in Antonio's face.

"I don't know but she did it," Antonio says, pointing at me.

If I never get another compliment in my life, it will not matter. Because I made the homies read that shit.

April 19

Tuesday rears its head, the sky thick with warning. We are teaching on the units today as we are on day three of the move.

There are two off-sight therapeutic camps run by the probation department, one for boys and one for girls. The qualifying factors are that the child have non-sexual offenses, be sentenced for a minimum of six months, and must be considered fixable in the eyes of probation. The boy's camp was constantly full. The girl's camp was not full and had never been. The girl's camp had been built to house thirty girls, but the population never got above eight. Since both the camp schools and the hall school depend on the money they receive from the government for each student enrolled, the girls camp was not able to cover the exorbitant costs needed to run the place. Someone had said the girls camp, between the staffing, the programs, and the lack of resident bodies, was costing the county about a million dollars a month to run.

As a result, the girl's camp was closing and the six girls currently living there were being transferred to the hall. Our staff did not think that it would be that much of an issue. The girls at camp had been at the hall before, we knew them all, and we assumed the girls wouldn't make that big of a deal of having to come back. And the girls didn't make an issue out of the transition, but the camp staff sure as hell did. The problem with most things isn't the kids, it's the adults.

With the girls from camp came their staff and all of their personalities. How well we could all get along if everyone just left their personality at home every day. We had assumed that the transitioning staff would try to blend in at the hall, try to make the shift as smoothly as possible. But from day one, the camp staff made it crystal clear to both the teachers and the hall staff that they were going to do their own thing. For starters, they refused to let their six girls live in the female housing unit. They took over another unit that is usually used in times of overflow, like right now. This caused the ten kids on that unit to be pushed out into other units, sending several of them in max capacity. The camp staff demanded that renovations be made to the unit to accommodate their six girls. They also said that their girls must travel with their own camp staff member at all time, be allowed to wear a separate uniform, have extra privileges like name-brand toiletries, and that the girls be seated separately from the other girls in every class. They had requested a separate teacher and a separate cook for the six camp girls as well, but probation and the school nixed those ideas due to budget issues. It was vividly clear that the camp staff had no intention of trying to get their girls to assimilate. Rather they were segregating their kids, making it clear that they did not like what was happening to them and that they would fight tooth and nail against acclimating. It was like someone who being rescued from drowning complaining that the rescue vessel wasn't to their liking and attempting to redecorate as soon as they finish coughing water up out of their lungs. To make matters worse, when the camp closed down, the school there did as well. So everything in the school came to us: every last book, desk, office supply, as well as an entire library. The whole school had been packed into boxes, dumped over the weekend into our library and copy room, leaving us to sort through the wreckage.

Today is the final step in this laborious process, the day that the girls physically move into their new surroundings and one of the managers at the hall had asked if we could teach on the units. His request was reasonable. After all, moving vans would be bringing in all of the camp furniture for the new unit. That would leave the delivery entrance open for a period of time, which posed a very real hazard. Open the gates and the monsters escape. Welcome to Jurassic Park.

I am taking roll when the call comes over the radio, "Code orange!" There is a fight going on. Mr. Robbins charges into the program room that doubles as a unit classroom, yelling, "Code! Take it down!"

The kids fall over themselves charging for their rooms, stumbling over chairs and one another. A few boys who are new and do not know yet what to do in these situations, either freeze in their seats, awaiting specific instruction or drop to the floor where they are trampled and tripped over by the more seasoned boys charging back to their cells.

I rush through the corridor that joins the unit I was on and the one in which the fight was happening. I get to the unit door in time to see one kicking and screaming boy being dragged away from another boy curled on the floor, coughing up blood. Twenty-five boys are sprawled across the floor on their stomachs, hands clasped behind their backs.

Two guards tackle the screaming boy, pinning him to the carpet and throwing handcuffs onto him, while another group of guards pry apart two other boys who have taken advantage of the moment to start another fight in the opposite corner of the room. The screaming boy is a relatively new Sureno and the boy coughing up blood is Jorge, who spasms and writhes on the floor like a downed live wire. The other two boys who had gotten into a separate fight are Kevin and another Sureno. Extra guards pour into the unit, filing the gaps between the boys on the floor, making sure no one tries to start anything else.

Mr. Addams, an elderly volunteer dance teacher, limps towards a chair.

"What happened?" I hiss to Jack who was watching impassively. He has been here longer than anyone and has seen way too many fights.

"Those two got into it and Mr. Addams tried to break them up. He got kicked in the knee pretty badly." He alternates sips from a Styrofoam cup of coffee with bites from a poppy-seed bagel, black specks falling to the floor.

One of the cardinal rules is that you do not, under any circumstances, get in-between two kids fighting. You sound the alarm and let the guards handle it. That is what they are trained for. But I understand the impulse to get children to stop hurting each other. On the outside, you would try to intervene, maybe even pull them apart. But in the hall you have to fight that gut reaction and just watch nature take its ugly course, much like wildlife photographers who must stand idle as the gazelle gets run down and ripped apart.

Mr. Addams rocks back and forth in a chair, holding his knee, his slack face white and grimacing. More guards pour into the unit, filling the spaces between the prone bodies littering the floor. The air is thick with adrenaline, everyone slightly breathless and wide-eyed. The towering figures of staff are like black icebergs, looming over a flat sea of blue bodies.

"No more school," Mr. Robbins limps by Jack and I, his face dripping with sweat. "Everyone is done for the day."

"You can't cancel school for everyone because of four kids!"

"Watch me," Mr. Robbins snarls, hobbling towards the door. And he was correct; he absolutely could and did. How do you punish ninety-six bystanders for the actions of four assailants? Is punishment a net that widely cast that even the errant porpoise entangled in a tuna-trolling line must pay the same price just because of their proximity?

"This is bull-shit," I grouse at Jack as we walk back down to the school department. From the other units, Sara and Ralph and Yvonne are also making their way back to home base. We are all on the losing team today.

"That's just how it is around here. They can justify anything if they say it is done in the name of safety and security." I can't decide if he has just seen so much that he accepts all eventualities with the calm acceptance of a Buddhist monk or if he has just learned over the years that you can't fight an avalanche.

"At a regular school, you wouldn't cancel every class just because of a fight. You are only supposed to punish the kids that are involved. What the hell kind of message does that send, that everyone is guilty and punishable just because they are here?"

"They are guilty, remember?" Sara chides, coming along beside us. "That's why they are here."

"Yea, they are guilty for something. But they already got punished for that. It's like there is no expiration date for punishment. If you are guilty of one thing, you are guilty of everything forever." I throw a box of oil pastels at my desk, the angry confetti of it spattering outwards, a rainbow .45 blast.

"Don't get too close to this," Yvonne warns me softly from the doorway. "You'll only get frustrated. We can't fight them. This is their house."

"Yea, well then I want to go home."

She purses her lips and gives me a look that is half pity and half understanding and leaves me to my petulance. Sitting behind my desk in my cavernous classroom, my eyes begin to sting. What the fuck am I doing here, beating on the walls of Jericho and expecting to make a dent? How do you fight an entire system when all you have are words and pencils and some idealistic aspirations? That hopelessness settles in my ribs again, a weighted ghost bird. I can't reach kids that I can't even see. Maybe I wouldn't feel this overwhelmingly helpless and spinning if I wasn't constantly losing students. This clawing, gnawing, writhing desperation that surges through the veins of every day; the knowledge that I have only an hour left in the life of a child. I need to somehow make that one hour mean something, if only I could reach some closed off and shut-down part in them. It's a desperate, constant ache like a ruptured molar. I guess I have become so used to it over the past seven months that I never saw it for what it was. Every day is someone's last day with me, my last chance to try and reach them, help them, show them something, make them think. Every day is my last chance.

April 24

Keeping writing interesting and challenging, yet accessible for a group of students that range in skill level from kids who have already graduated high school to eighth graders who cannot read the word 'quality' is very difficult. I have read more books on writing prompts than I care to recall and the suggestions usually range from the inane and juvenile (describe a world where it rains ice cream) to topics that touch on experiences that are simply not in my student's wheelhouse (write about the last time your family took a tropical vacation). My students have the interests and where-with-all of any other child their age, but their writing and reading comprehension skills are on average at about an eighth grade level. I usually end up spending at least an hour or two every night creating daily writing prompts that are both engaging yet accessible.

Every kid has written about what their perfect day would be. Prompts like that are boring the first time around and are mind-numbingly tedious by the second. Quotes and song lyrics have been consistently successful in starting dialogue and pulling some remarkable writing out of them. Today, I gave the students the following chunk of dialogue from *Schindler's List* to muse over before writing:

Schindler: Why (do they) they fear us?
Goeth: We have the power to kill, that's why they fear us.
Schindler: They fear us because we have the power to kill arbitrarily. A man commits a crime, he should know better. We have him killed and we feel pretty good about it. Or we kill him ourselves and we feel even better. That's not power, though, that's justice. That's different than power. Power is when we have every justification to kill – and we don't.

This quote takes significant explanation, much more so than I had expected. Roughly half of my students had little to no idea what the Holocaust was. I try my best to summarize five years of hell into five minutes of background.

"What are the SS?" asks Juan.

"The SS were basically like an army for Nazi Germany. SS stood for Schutzstaffel which means Protection Squadron."

"They sound alright. I mean if they were protecting people, that's good, right?"

"They said they were protecting people. They were actually killing people but they did it like they were doing it for the benefit of the German people," Antonio says.

"So the SS was bad?" Jorge looks confused.

"They were an army that wanted to wipe out a whole group of people. Not even just Jewish people but gay people and people with disabilities, too." I explain.

"Why did they say they were protecting people?"

"Same reason why anyone lies, I guess. They want someone to believe something other than the truth."

"Why the hell would someone be a part of that shit?" asks Jorge, to no one in particular. "Fuck the SS and all that Nazi shit. How could anybody be so stupid to get involved with something like that?"

I feel my devil horns starting to poke through my scalp. This is too perfect of an opportunity to pass up. "A lot of people say that the Nazis were just a really big, successful gang."

"Hell no. That's some bullsh...I mean that's false. How can you compare the Nazis to any Latino gang?" Jesus demands. "It's totally different."

"Well, let's write it out." I uncap my pen and make a giant T-chart on the board, writing Nuestra Familia on one column and Nazi on the other. "Let's identify the things that make up a gang and see if both have them. You guys down?"

They can shut this down right here if they wanted to. The boys glance around at each other before Juan agrees, "Go for it, but I think you will see that you are wrong."

"I don't mind being wrong but I want to know the facts either way. What does a gang have?"

The boys are so excited to be asked a question they know the answer to. A cause, soldiers, enemies, territory, and symbols go up on the board.

"What was the Nazi's cause?"

"They wanted to kill the Jews and take over Europe," Marco calls out.

"Kill the enemy and take over territory. So who were their

people and territory?"

"Germans, right? And like anyone who wanted what they wanted. They started in Germany. But they wanted to take over all of Europe, right?" Antonio offers.

"Exactly." I point to the final category: symbols and colors.

"I saw a video of them. They always wore that weird cross thing with the bent arms. And their flag was red and white and black. And they had a goofy-ass walk that they did," Kevin adds.

I add these to the chart and pointed to the Nuestra Familia side of it. I don't need to say or write anything. The boys' faces fall. They see it.

"Oh shit, " mumbles Jose, his eyes opening like a clenched blossom finally hit with sunlight.

"It's the same. Fuck, it's the same." Juan sucks his breath in through his teeth.

"Nah, Miss Wehr, you can't play us like that. We ain't no Nazis," Carlos snaps angrily.

"Play you like what? All I did was write down the answers you gave me for the categories we decided on together. These are your words and thoughts."

"But we aren't like that. You know us. You can't say that we are like them." Juan's voice is almost pleading. This is a truth too heavy to carry.

"Aren't like what?"

"Like...THAT! THEM!" His eyes solar-flare and spittle flies from his trembling lips.

"Let's look at what's the same, shall we? You both have a name, territory you claim, a cause you fight for, people you want to kill, and symbols that represent you. Seems like Latino gags have a lot in common with the Nazis."

"We are not Nazis!" Juan is raging now.

"I am not saying you are. I don't think that the Nazis would take on a Latino foot solider. But aren't there a lot of similarities between your gang and the Nazis?"

I am stepping out of my role as an educator. No curriculum would ever contain or condone this type of discussion, but I am fed up with my students defending their gang lifestyles like it was something noble. They need to see just what exactly they are a part of, even if it made them really angry. I don't care if they hate me for it. If that's the price I have to pay for getting them to see this, then so be it.

"No, there isn't. I mean they wanted to kill all the Jewish people. We don't want to kill the Jewish people," Carlos says.

"You just want to kill the Southerners."

"Yea, but that's different."

"How?"

"I don't know! It just is!"

"It's different cause they want to kill us, too. The Jews didn't want to kill the Nazis," Marco adds calmly, always my voice of reason.

"That is absolutely correct. And just to clarify, I am not singling out Nuestra Familia here. The same goes for MS-13 or Latin Kings or the Bloods and the Crips. There is no good gang. You are all responsible because you all participate. But every gang has a lot of the same components. Modern street gangs and World War II Nazis have a cause and soldiers and territory and symbols they claim."

"But the Nazis took over countries. We are just trying to defend our hood," explains Juan.

"That's the whole issue! It's cyclical. An enemy wanders into your neighborhood. You kill him. Then one of his homies kills you. Then one of your homies kills that homie. And so forth. All because of revenge and territory. The Nazis wanted to enact revenge on a perceived enemy: the Jews. And they wanted the power of running more countries."

"You are making it sound like we want all this territory," Carlos throws his arms out wide like he is center-stage in a jailhouse tableaux vivant of *The Last Supper*.

"You want more territory, right? You guys get into turf wars. The Nazis did it on a country-size scale, but you are doing the same thing. You are just starting small, with city blocks and streets."

"We aren't going to start no killing camps," Jorge growls, flicking his wrist angrily in my direction.

"You are right. You won't because you don't have the manpower and you would get shut down pretty quick. But if you could find a way to kill your enemy quicker and in larger quantities, I think you guys would go for it."

198

"It's different. You just don't get it, " grumbles Kevin, crossing his arms.

"Oh you are right. I don't understand the gang lifestyle or mentality. I never have and I never will. But I do know when two things have something in common. Or in this case, a few things."

"How can you do this to us?" Juan whispers, his voice cracked with betrayal. "You said that you loved us."

"It's because I love you that I am saying this to you! Do you think loving someone means being okay with whatever the hell they are doing, even if it's killing them?"

"But if you love us, you love all of us, every part. You can't turn your back on us like that."

"And I am not turning my back. Do you see me going anywhere? I will love you and encourage you and help you and support you as much as I can, but this part of you I absolutely despise. I love all of you more than I can put into words and that's why this destroys me. You are hurting someone I love."

"What are you trying to say, Miss Wehr?" Antonio speaks slowly and calmly.

"I am saying that what you are doing is wrong. Killing is killing. Killing one person is the same as killing many. The Talmud says that if you destroy one soul, it is the same as destroying a whole world."

"How is killing one person like killing the whole world?" Juan is cautiously approaching a cliff that he is afraid to look down from.

"You ended that person's whole world, didn't you?"

No one says another word for the rest of the period. We stare at one another over the chasm that has opened between us.

April 30

"Should parents always tell their children the truth?"

"If my kid asked me where babies come from, I would just tell them a baby is a gift from God. I don't want to talk about sex with my kid," says Jorge.

"What if your kid heard you and your wife having sex? What would you say?" asks Juan.

"I would just say the TV was on too loud," mutters Jorge, his cheeks flushing red. "Or you can say you were wrestling. That way it's not a whole lie."

"What about adoption? Would you tell your kid if they were adopted?" Jose glances around the room for a few seconds before continuing, "Cause I just found that I was adopted last week. I am sixteen years old and I had to find out that the people who I call mom and dad are not my parents. Where I was born, what happened to my parents, the age when I was adopted, everything! And it wasn't even my parents who told me. My probation officer did."

"But aren't you happy that you know the truth?" asks Juan.

"Course I am happy I know, but this was a fucked up way to find out! My adoptive parents never told me that I was adopted when I was eight months old or that my mom died when I was a month old or that my dad was an alcoholic who committed suicide in jail last year. Everything was a lie! They said they were trying to protect me but I would have rather they told me than having to find out from a probation officer in jail. The system took me from my parents cause they were drug addicts but the people I got stuck with are also drug addicts. They took me from one bad place and put me in another bad one. You know how I found out about my dad? My probation officer showed me a picture of my dad's dead body hanging in his jail cell and told me that I was going to end up like him. I had never even seen my dad before and the first time I see him, he is dead and purple and hanging from the ceiling of a fucking cell."

"My mom lied to me all the time. When I was little, she used to tell me that I was the reason why she didn't have a job. When my dad got murdered, she just told me he was on vacation. For two years. I had to find out on my own when my uncle got drunk and let it slip one night," says Antonio.

"My mom didn't tell me that my dad went to prison when I was in kindergarten. I mean, I get why she wanted to protect me, but at least if I knew he was locked up, I would know his not being around was not a choice. For years, I always thought my dad had just abandoned me," says Jesus.

"I guess, we understand why some parents lie to their kids about some stuff. But having all been lied to, I think we would prefer to just know the hard facts and deal with it. My dad would tell me my mom was at work when she would disappear for days at a time. I was little but I still knew that he was lying. I didn't know where she was or what she was doing, but I could tell it was bad," Kevin says softly.

"Is it okay to lie to protect someone's feelings?" I ask.

"Yes....sometimes, " Juan answers.

"No. Never." Jose counters.

The two boys turn and look at one another, shocked and surprised that the person who usually agreed with everything they said actually had a different point of view.

"What do you mean 'no, never'?" Juan demands.

"Can you phrase that more respectfully?" I ask.

"Sorry. Jose, I don't fucking agree with you."

"I think a man has to be about his word, one hundred percent. Remember when we talked about honesty last week and how your word is your bond? I believe that. If you don't have your word, and you don't have the respect that comes with people knowing you keep it real, then you have nothing."

"I hear you. But say you got a kid and you get locked up. You want your kid to know you are locked up? Shouldn't you just tell them you're working or something so they don't worry about you?"

"My kid is gonna find out eventually. And then they will hate me for lying to them."

"Your kid isn't going to hate you! They will understand. You did it to protect them. They will forgive you," Antonio adds.

"You forgive your mom for lying to you about your pops?" Jose asks softly.

"Yea, I forgive her. She did what she thought was best. Sometimes you gotta do bad stuff for good reasons."

"Like Robin Hood! Isn't that right, Miss Wehr?" Marco adds.

"Yes, Robin Hood did bad things like stealing, but he did it for an honorable reason. Everyone has their reasons for lying. There may be good reasons or selfish reasons or even fearful reasons."

"Fearful? I ain't never lied cause I was scared," Jorge sneers.

"You ever lied to a cop?" I ask, slightly bemused.

"Yea."

"Why?"

"Cause I didn't want to get arrested."

"You were afraid you were going to get arrested. So you lied out of fear."

"I wasn't afraid!" Jorge is incensed already. This kid can go from zero to red zone quicker than any kid I have ever met.

"Homie, we are all scared when the cops roll up. None of us want to come back," Jose's voice is a level louder than normal and he is gesturing sharply with his hands.

"I am not scared! Of cops or nobody!" Jorge folds his arms to indicate that this was final.

"Shit, I'm scared," Eduardo says.

"Big surprise." Jorge rolls his eyes.

"What you scared of?" Jose asks.

"Of dying. Of getting shot. Of disappointing my family. Of failing. Of being like my dad."

"We are all scared of that stuff," Antonio says gently.

"A real man ain't supposed to be scared of nothing," Jorge is muttering, his gaze glued to a floor tile a few feet in front of him.

"Fear can actually be helpful. Fear is what keeps us from walking in front of cars or doing any number of dangerous things. If everyone didn't have some fear, our species would have ended thousands of years ago." I want the boys to see fear as any other emotion, to understand that it is not a weakness to be afraid. Some of the strongest people are terrified.

"Growing up, everyone always told me not to be scared of nothing. I used to cry about the dark cause I was scared of it. I guess I got hella annoying so my parents would hit me when I got scared or sad or cried. After a while I stopped getting scared and I just got angry instead. Now everything makes me mad," Jesus murmurs.

"Shit, my step-dad did that, too! That's what you are supposed to do when you got a son. You gotta toughen him up! You gotta make a man out of him! A real man ain't soft! Your dad wouldn't hit you if he didn't want the best for you. He was trying to keep you from being queer." Jorge has twisted around in his seat and is jabbing his finger at Jesus as he spits out the words.

"Being scared doesn't make you queer," Eduardo's voice is harder than usual and a bit louder. The boys turn towards Eduardo, mildly shocked at his defiance.

"It makes you more like a girl and that's one step closer to being a gay than I will ever take. Only girls and gays are scared of shit. Which one are you?" Jorge's tone is reaching a dark and ugly place.

"Jorge," I say, holding up my hand. He gives me a mea culpa gesture with his own and sinks back into his chair, lips folded into themselves like an angry envelope. The class is silent for a moment.

"I think we should write about this," Antonio says. "We are not going to handle it any other way."

And they began to write like their lives depended on it.

May 3

The kids are sadly one-minded when it comes to literature. The girls want to read *Twilight* and anything having to do with paranormal romance. Since I refuse to keep literary soft-core emotional porn for hormonal teenagers in my classroom, the girls are sadly out of luck.

The boys are equally single-minded. They want books about gangs, the bloodier the better. My copies of *Always Running* and *Monster* were the first to be stolen. Occasionally I will get a student who thinks they are being very clever by asking for *The Art of War* or *The Prince*. They want to improve their manipulation tactics and war strategy, but are elevating it above a street gang level.

Jesus was even more candid in regards to his intentions when he approached me yesterday. "I want to be a sociopath. Do you have any books that can teach me how to be a sociopath?"

"What a shame. I just lent *Sociopaths for Dummies* to another kid."

"Nah, seriously. I want to know how to manipulate people. Do you have any books on how to do that?"

"I would ask why, but I am afraid that would make me an accessory." Scanning the bookshelves, I tried to find a classic I could foist on him. There it was, dusty from a year of none-use.

"*The Screwtape Letters?* What's this?" Jesus looked at me suspiciously, like I had just handed him a ticking box.

"It's about two devils discussing how to take over the human soul."

"Sweet!"

Today, I encounter a disgruntled Jesus in the hallway and ask him how he liked the book.

"I liked it until it got me in trouble. I tried one of the mind control tricks on staff and I got in trouble for manipulating a guard."

"Kind of your own fault, don't you think?"

"They also searched my room and took my *Art of Seduction*."

"Jesus, you are in jail. Who exactly are you going to seduce?"

"I won't be in here forever and I gotta stay on point. It sucks that they got all bent outta shape over this."

"With great power comes great responsibility, I guess."

"Spiderman never had to deal with this shit."

Last period the energy is high and fragile. The boys are antsy and across the room, legs are bouncing quickly beneath desks.

"Antonio just found out he's leaving in a few days," Juan crows, reaching forward and clasping Antonio's shoulders. Antonio does his touchdown arms, a broad grin spread across his face.

"You're leaving us? I'm so happy!"

"Oh, that's nice," Antonio rolls his eyes.

"You know what I mean. I love seeing all of you guys every day but I also like knowing that you are going out to make your way in the world. Are you excited?"

"I'm excited to be with my family again. And I'm going to sign up for community college. Gonna be a man of business." He looks so proud of himself for having a plan. Definitely more hopeful than I have seen him this time around.

"I am glad you are thinking about your future. Very fitting actually because today we are going to write about our pasts."

"Oh shit," laughs Juan. "Miss Wehr, you trying to get some new charges thrown at us?"

"Just say allegedly," Kevin explains. "That means you might have done it and you might not have. My lawyer told me that."

"We are going to go farther back. Back to when you were ten years old. I want you to write a letter to your ten year old self."

"Saying what exactly?" Jesus asks.

"Whatever you want to say. If you could somehow go back in time, knowing what you know now and have a sit-down with your ten year old self, what would you say? Would you give advice? Warnings? Help? Hope?"

Twenty minutes slide by in complete silence as they pour themselves into their papers. This is furious writing, deadly serious, aching and grasping. They are writing like they are hanging on a cliff. There is a desperation here so large no vessel in the world could accommodate it.

"I can't write my thoughts fast enough," Marco whispers, his pencil snapping under the weight of his death grip. "It's like there isn't enough words in my mind to say what I need to say."

"I need to read this. Right now, Miss Wehr. I have to read mine." Juan's voice is desperate and shaking. "We all need to read ours."

There is an urgency here I cannot turn my back on. They need to speak and I need to hear every word of it. These boys have spent their whole lives being talked to, talked at. But had anyone ever listened? Hearing this, agreeing to hold it with them was a huge task and I am not sure that I am strong enough for this. I can barely handle my own sorrows and stones. Understanding a hurting person, in a deep and visceral sense, means that you hurt with them, too.

Dear 10-Year-Old Juan,

I understand it's hard to grow up with your dad always being on drugs and asking yourself who is going to teach me the ways of life? Seek help. Everyone needs help. Whatever you do, respect others. Have feelings for other people. Respect their belongings. If you are having money problems, don't ruin innocent people who work hard for their possessions. Don't sell drugs because you'll be killing them slowly. You need to care about people. You aren't mad at people you don't know. You are mad at your dad. So don't take out your anger on someone's face and try to ruin their lives the way your dad did to you.

Dear 10-Year-Old Antonio,

You are going to kill yourself. You don't care, but in reality you do. I hope you look at this and take it all in and understand that I am trying to save your life. I know it is hard to think that anybody can get to what is inside of you. It is hard to think that you are capable of anything you will do. Dad will be gone, but don't let that shit bring you down. You are going to feel like you are stuck in a shell and it's getting too small and you can't find a new one.

Dear 10-Year-Old Jesus,

I messed up my life doing drugs and gangbanging. I know it isn't too late, but it's so hard to change my life. Don't give up like me. I gave up on myself and my whole life turned to darkness. I hope that one day I will change and be the opposite of the person I am today. I will be released soon but that I will never get that time back. I wish I had the time.

Dear 10-Year-Old Jose,

If I was able to go back to your age, I would in a second. It's up to you if you want to start doing drugs and drinking. I won't tell you when you are going to be asked, but it's your choice. Everything will be about choices. Your emotions shouldn't always be hidden, either. One important thing: everything dad says is actually true. And just study him. You are what he was when he was young. Watch out for the world. Oh and you won't be with the same girl that you are now, so have fun.

Dear 10-Year-Old Jorge,

Half the situations you were in didn't have to go down they way they did. Some friends will be loyal and some are just waiting for you to turn around to stab you. Fuck what everyone else is doing. I don't care how tough you are, life can beat you to your knees and keep you there permanently if you let it. But it isn't always about how hard you hit. It's about how hard you can get hit and keep going. Cowards do that and that isn't you.

Dear 10-Year-Old Kevin,

My whole life I wanted to be the strong guy who wasn't afraid of nothing or no one. I went to jail the first time in seventh grade. I didn't think I was as bad as people said I was. But look where it got me. I guess they were right.

Dear 10-Year-Old Marco,

Your mom will never be there for you. She will always love drugs more than you. I know you want her to come and take you with her, but don't learn to love her. She will be another issue in your life that you do not need.

Dear 10-Year-Old Eduardo,

You are in fifth grade and you already feel like your life sucks. Your life will become so much worse. Your mom's boyfriend starts fucking with drugs and beating your mom. You feel helpless, frozen, useless, like a bitch. It's not your fault. Part of the reason is because you don't tell him you love him. Maybe if you showed him a little more love, things would change. You have to be the man of the house because you are the only sober one. You start doing any drugs you can find so people will stop depending on you. You have to live in and you never feel at home. You lose hope in everything. You used to believe in God but then you hate him for everything that you have been through. You start not to care about anything or anyone. I hope that you can still be that one kid who loves life and is scared of dying. Cause right now, I feel like giving up on life.

May 10

The girls straggle in, drowsy and disoriented following lunch. The carb-intensive meals here shove the kids into walking comas. Dazed and smiling sleepily, they silently wander to the supply table, grabbing their folders and pencils.

Tessa lays her head down on her desk, which is getting to be a tighter fit due to her growing belly. I begin to explain the writing prompt that I gave to the boys yesterday.

"What did the boys have to say?" Vanessa asks, slowly scratching her ankle, revealing a monitoring bracelet. She must be getting out soon if they have already hooked up the electric leash.

"They had a lot of powerful insights. I am sure you will have some similar ones." I am choosing my words carefully. Vanessa is dating Jose and she often asks what they wrote about to see if he mentioned her in his writing. He has yet to write about her, but I avoid telling her that directly.

"Did they wish they could change anything?" Miranda asks.

"Absolutely. Doesn't everyone? People who say they have no regrets are in denial. Everyone wishes something, even a little thing, had worked out differently."

"I wish so much of my life had gone differently," Miranda whispers, shaking her head. "But I can't let myself have regrets. If I did, it would be so much and so many, I don't think I could go on. I have to feel like it was all for a purpose. If it wasn't, if it was just pain for no reason.... damn. I can't even let my mind go there."

The boy's twenty minutes is eclipsed by the ladies thirty minutes, all writing hunched over their papers as if being close to the words will protect them.

Dear 10-Year-Old Miranda,

Life isn't always going to be as great as it is now. Being the older you, I have seen it all. I am locked up and away from family due to the bad decisions I have made. As you grow, you are going to think you know everything, but you don't. Soon you will have too much pride to ask anyone for help and later in life you are going to find yourself all alone. Don't be in such a rush to grow up. You have to forgive and come to peace with your past. Don't let it define you. Let it be what gives you knowledge and makes you a stronger you. Release all the pain and anger you have. It's not taking you anywhere.

Dear 10-Year-Old Shawna,

Instead of telling you what not to do, I will tell you to follow your heart. There are things that we must go through in life, even if they feel like never-ending pain. You will come into many people's lives and you will change each one forever. That's why people are drawn to you and even after lengths of time, when they see you they will light up. You are in for some amazing blessings, lessons, and pain.

Dear 10-Year-Old Tessa,

You've been through a lot, seen things most ten year olds have only witnessed on TV or in a movie. You're a very smart girl who gets A's and B's to feel loved by your family. Everyone around you does drugs and you see how it makes them change. Don't be like that. Don't make life harder than it already is. You recently had a home invasion done to you and a gun put to your head. Forget that ever happened. Erase it from your memory. Don't let it phase you. Revenge is pointless, remember that. If a man hits you, leave. Don't stay because you think he loves you and is sorry. If he loves you, he wouldn't hurt you.

Dear 10-Year-Old Alexa,

You are going to experience a lot of pain in the years to come. I want you to prepare yourself for the tragedy and pain you will experience. Do not push away the people who actually love you because eventually they will not want to be around you. You will lose your parents, but that does not mean you should give up.

Dear 10-Year-Old Vanessa,

At ten you think you know all there is to know about life. You get pulled apart from your family and you join a gang. Sooner or later you will realize you made some bad decisions and you need to pay for the consequences. Do what's right and don't be afraid of who you are. Drugs and gangs ain't nothing to leave easy. You might gain respect in the streets, but nowhere else.

What strikes me the most when I hear the girl's work compared to the boys is the difference in tone. While the boys took a more lecturing, authoritative tone with their younger selves, the girl's tone was much more compassionate and nurturing. The boys chastised and warned their younger selves about future stumbling blocks and gave direct, but very poignant advice. The girls cradled their young selves, whispering soothing words of encouragement and acceptance. The girls could see how precious their little selves were, how in need they were of hope and affirmation. Just knowing that they were okay, that they were strong and they were seen could have made a world of difference.

May 15

The rain is falling sideways, a bitter wind whipping it against me as I trudge up to the cellblocks. Between the cumbersomeness of my pea coat and the two sweaters under it, I bear more than a passing resemblance to Randy from *A Christmas Story*, stumbling through the doorway into the unit, books falling from my arms.

Mr. Robbins comes out from behind the guard station, laughing, "And to think some people can't do that gracefully."

"I minored in awkward entrances during my undergrad."

"Miss Wehr!" Antonio is calling out through his cell door across the room. "Can I talk to you?"

"You don't have to talk to him," Mr. Robbins says. "You and I both know he is nothing but trouble."

"I don't know that," I reply flatly. I hate when people tell me what I know. But honestly all I want to do is leave the claustrophobia of the cellblock and go get ready for that day. Part of me just wanted to tell him to talk to me in class. Maybe he was just trying to get out of his cell for a few moments. I turned to call out for him to just talk to me first period, but his eyes froze me: please don't wait for me.

We walk silently to the program room. Antonio shuts the door behind us and pulls two chairs into the center of the room. Settling into one, he slowly rubs his hands together. He is trying to work up the nerve to say something. He glances up at me, his torso bent so far into his lap that he is almost folded in two.

"I am going to leave California. I talked to my uncle and he said he would pay for me to move to Florida. He's in the Air Force, married with three kids. He said I can stay with him until I get a job and get on my feet."

This wasn't a vacate the premises notice, this was a warning of the rapture. "Are you saying what I think you are saying? Are you going to leave your gang?"

He nods, his hands trembling slightly.

"Oh my God. Are you being honest?"

Raising himself up, he squares off with me eye to eye. Voice shaking with the power of its message, he croaks, "I swear on everything I love."

212

"Can I ask why?" I am apprehensive with the beauty of this. Nothing this good can really happen in these walls, can it?

"Because this ain't no life. I have been thinking and every time I ever got in trouble, it was because of something I did with or for the gang. All of my problems come from that. Maybe if I left, if I stopped, I could do some good. Get a job, get married and have babies, be around to watch them grow up."

"This is such a huge, wonderful thing. I don't even know what to do with this information. What made you change your mind?"

"Don't laugh, but it was a dream I had. I dreamed I was posting up with some homies and this car cruised by and just started unloading at us. My homies hid but I got shot in the heart. And I died alone and bleeding in the gutter. Miss Wehr, I don't want to die."

"You know that if you keep doing what you are doing, you probably will end up with a bullet in you." Telling a child that they are going to die is too large of a thing for the morning.

"I know. I want to be a great artist one day. I want to have kids and be a good dad. Not like my dad." There is a moment of silence between us. His hands are still shaking, knees bouncing nervously. He nods, the shaking spreading up into his arms. "So that's what I wanted to tell you; I am getting out."

"There should be a new word for proud because what I am feeling is so much bigger than that. But why tell me?"

"Cause you never turned your back on me, even when I fucked up in class and was disrespectful and lazy. I gave up on myself a long time ago, but you never did. And that made me realize that maybe there is something in me that's worth saving. You always treated me like a person, not like I was just a gang member or a criminal. And what you said about how you love all of us, but you won't support our lifestyle. No one ever said anything like that to me. I thought you were just being mean but then I realized it was the nicest thing anyone has ever done for me." He stops speaking, but he isn't done. There was something he wasn't telling me and the lack of it hung between us.

"What's the other reason you are telling me this?" This feels like the beginnings of a suicide note.

Antonio shifts in his chair, crosses his ankles and then uncrossing them. He casts an eye out of the window towards the cells. Jorge stands at the window in his door, grim and foreboding as the reaper. He can't possibly hear us, but his eyes glitter darkly with understanding.

"When I leave, I gotta get..." He makes a weird hand movement, like a stutter in gesture form.

"You have to get jumped out, right?"

"Blood in and blood out. So I wanted you to know, in case something happens, this was why."

"You mean in case they kill you?"

"Yea, I want you to know it was because I was trying to do something good. If I die, it's because I was trying to make my life better for once, not worse."

"Can't you just leave without telling anyone? Skip the whole being assaulted and possibly being killed part of this?"

"I may be a dropout, but I ain't no punk. I have to do this with honor. I can't explain why to you. Maybe if I had ever gone to English class on the outs, I would have words for this. But I don't think you would get it. It's going to be bad enough that I am leaving. My friends aren't going to talk to me anymore. They are going to want to kill me. So I am going to be alone for a long time, but if I have to be alone, I would rather be alone with honor."

I decide to let it alone. I don't approve of the way he is leaving, but this is his exodus and he had to do it his own way. "Can I give you a hug?" I ask him.

We hug, the buzz of cell doors and radio crackle filling the vast emptiness around us.

"You are the first person besides my mom who has ever hugged me." He rubs his nose on his sleeve like a tired child and for a moment he is all of five years old. The outside of his splits and he is just his smallest and purest self. His need for love and acknowledgment and protection and comfort is just as glowing and all consuming as anyone else's. He doesn't deserve less because of his mistakes; he requires more.

Looking back over the past few weeks, there were some big signs that something was happening. Antonio had started to sitting apart from the other boys in class, virtually cutting off contact

214

between him and the rest of the Northerners. In gang society, staying physically close with your fellow members is not just a security measure, but also a public statement as to where your allegiance lay. At first I had chalked it up to a rift between the boys, but I now understood what Antonio was doing: he was taking a stance through distance.

While preparing for class this morning, I realized I had made a horrible wardrobe choice. I was wearing a necklace of large, light blue beads. The aversion to the color red that Surenos possess is matched only by the Nortenos disgust with blue. The boys stream in over the course of a few minutes, filling the left side of the classroom. Antonio sits alone in the first row of the right side of the classroom. Jorge mutters something to Carlos, shooting a glance at Antonio. As I am taking roll, the clasp of my necklace snaps and the whole blue mess falls to the floor.

"Oh for corn's sake," I sigh, scooping it up. "Are any of you guys good with fixing clasps?"

Most of them were very good with their hands, having fixed my electric pencil sharpener and picking my cabinet locks with a bobby pin when I lost my keys. But they all stare back at me, glassy-eyed. They would not fix something blue that was broken. It was condemned by its color.

Antonio raises his hand. "Here, let me have a look at it."

I hand him the necklace and the silence somehow gets even deeper. The boys watch Antonio, waiting to see what he would do. He must have felt their gazes on the back of his neck because he begins to tremble and sweat as his fingers work over the clasp. In a minute that stretched endlessly in both directions, he holds up the fixed necklace.

The older boys, Jorge and Jesus and Carlos, lower their heads in disgust. Eduardo and Marco look confused, as if someone suddenly changed the rules and they no longer knew what game they were playing.

No one talks to Antonio for the rest of the class. The divide is not just the rows of empty desks between them. Antonio was making a stand, pulling back from the biggest part of his own identity. I cannot even fathom how difficult this must be. When you remove your core, you are left imbalanced and empty. But like detox, it was the first necessary, painful step to salvation.

I have had people tell me that I am these kid's only hope. It's not true. They are their own hope. They just don't know it yet.

May 16

During lunch we find out the fight that had closed the school this morning hadn't been an ordinary fight. Normally one kid will try to get his stripes, meaning respect, from fellow gang members by jumping a rival. Nine times out of ten, it's a Norteno jumping a Sureno. There are twenty Nortenos for every Sureno in here and they take a mean advantage of the odds. Fights normally follow the same format; one kid jumps the other, gets a few hits in, and yells a few gang-related terms before he is tackled by a guard. If it's a bit more coordinated, two or three fights may break out simultaneously so that the maximum amount of damage can be done before the staff takes control of the mess.

Mr. Robbins comes down to brief us on the incident. Today he is the acting manager, as there is no actual one on. He is nervous, fidgeting with the cuffs, badge, and radio on his belt. Just in this past year, his waist has expanded and the bits of gray at his temples have spread towards the back of his head. His eyes look heavy and puffy, the whites slightly bloodshot.

"I wanted to come and explain to you all what happened. The planning that went into this assault makes it a particularly disturbing situation. One of our Nortenos took it upon himself to assault a Sureno as retaliation for his assault against another Norteno a few weeks ago. He broke off a three-inch piece of hard plastic from one of the dinner trays and sharpened it into a shiv on the edge of his bunk. Last night when the boys came out for dinner, the Northerner charged the Southerner."

"Oh my god! Is he okay?" Yvonne gasps.

"He will be okay. He is in the hospital. Thankfully he had the wherewithal to tuck his head down so only the side of his face was sliced open instead of his throat. They had to stitch him up from jaw to eye, but he will be okay. Aside from having a pretty gruesome scar. Any questions? Okay, enjoy the rest of your lunch."

"He's going to have to change his gang name to Scarface," Jack says, shaking his head into his turkey sandwich.

The aggression between rival gang members is always present, but in an institution it's magnified due to the forced proximity of everyone. The kids who make it a point to stay in their own neighborhoods and on their own territory while on the outs are now forced to share a living unit with their sworn enemy. Sometimes they are even sharing a wall. And if the secretaries mess up their group placements, they sometimes end up in the same classroom. That last one is definitely something you want to avoid, at least in theory.

But in here, there are no guns. And the worst that could happen, aside from the occasional face-slashing incident, is that they would get a few punches in before the fight would break up. Some staff hypothesize that this is exactly the reason why the kids start fights so often. In here, a kid can get a few punches in, earn some respect from the homies, maybe he will get a black eye or something, and then the guards will pull it apart. They don't have to worry about tangling with someone who has a .45 shoved into his waistband in juvie. Kids today seem scared to lose so they bring a gun to what should be a fistfight.

These past few days have been lopsided and unsettling. Antonio was released and while the group is a bit less vocal for the loss, it is also missing the fun chaos of him. My mind wanders to him from time to time. I wonder if he is well and thriving or if he is struggling and suffering. It's so hard to have a piece of your heart out there, walking through the world unprotected. I don't know how parents can even breathe.

Realizing that it has been a few weeks since I have done something that irritates the staff, I decide to try an experiment today. I want to see if a Norteno and a Sureno can work together. The worse that can happen is that they fight and that happens even when we try to keep them separate. This was undoubtedly the worst possible time for me to try this experiment, but I was never any good at timing anyways.

We are teaching on the units after lunch so the staff could be there to take down anyone who tried to start a retaliation assault. After passing out the assignment and pencils, I inform the kids that the first two done with their work could break open the Memory game for the first time. My two fastest workers in this group are Marco and Alex, a Norteno and a Sureno, respectively. Since we are on the units, the students have all come out together, but the guards are seating the boys according to gang affiliation. All of the Surenos are at the back few tables, flanked by extra guards. The kids tear through their work, racing with one another to complete their packets.

Alex raises his hand to show he is done. I give him the nod to go over to the empty table a few feet away from the group and set the game up. Eagerly, he rips open the plastic and begins shuffling the tiles. Second hand up. Marco is done.

His face falls when he notices who he would be playing. He gestures furtively for me to come to him. "I can't play him," he whispers softly, glancing out the corner of his eye at Alex who has taken notice of what is going down.

Alex is sitting as straight as a scarecrow, his huge shaved head balanced precariously on his muscular shoulders. His tattooed fists are clenched. The Memory pieces lay in front of him, unflipped.

"Why not?"

"Cause he's a Southerner."

"So?"

"So nothing. I just can't."

"You don't want to play the first round?"

"It's not that. My homies wouldn't like it. And staff wouldn't like it neither."

"Let me worry about staff. They can yell at me for sending you over there if they want to. And your friends may not like it if you play him, but you would get respect if you won, wouldn't you?" I am betting a lot on this. Vegas has never seen such high stakes.

"I guess so." He stands, nodding to his fellow Nortenos who have been watching this whole exchange, and crosses to the metal lunch table where Alex is seated. Two of the guards began to charge across the room.

Taking my job into my hands, I step in front of them. "Please, I am begging you. Give it a second."

"This isn't smart," Mr. Robbins mutters.

"You are probably right," I agree.

Marco and Alex sit opposite one another. They look at one another dead in the eye, their respective body language a mirror image. No one is talking and the boys have all stopped working. The whole building is holding its breath. Marco reaches out and flips over one tile. Then another one. The entire housing unit exhales. Juan and Jose look like they have just seen a spaceship for the first time. The only one who refuses to look over there is Jorge. He keeps his head down, lips folded into a livid line.

"Nice work. You're insane," Mr. Robbins chuckles.

"Memory is a dangerous thing." I smile. "It just goes to show we don't know what anyone can do until we make them do what they thought they couldn't."

"Is that available stitched on a pillow?"

"Oh, shut up."

Marco and Alex are taking turns and keeping their hands to themselves. No gang signs are being thrown up, no one is yelling at anyone. Granted, neither one of them are talking at all. Yet they are still sitting at the same table, interacting peacefully. Still a move in the right direction. To the untrained eye, they look like two teenagers playing a game, albeit in matching sweatshirts.

May 28

Tension has been mounting in the girl's class. The girls who were moved over from the camp are at odds with the other girls, especially since two of them are fighting over Jorge. Never mind that he is two units over from them, a known womanizer, and a hardened gang member. Apparently in the alternate universe that is the hall, these are positive attributes. Today, the girls have grumbled and snipped their way through their classes, spitting out more snide asides than a Neil Simon play.

Their writing assignment has to do with the controversial rights of the incarcerated: tax-dollar funded surgeries, cable access, conjugal visits. The other classes had written and shared in under fifteen minutes. The girls take this assignment down a dark and personal tangent.

"I don't think the death penalty should be around at all. I think everyone should have their case reviewed before the parole board every ten or so years," Alexa says, her bird-like legs bent up beneath her.

Alexa is one of the more practical students. She doesn't let emotions cloud her judgment, isn't afraid to play devil's advocate to the rest of the girl's consensus on any and all topics, and has made more enemies than friends while in here as a result of said behavior.

"Hell no! If you kill someone, you should do life. That's it!" Vanessa was very quick to pronounce on any topic including those she knew nothing about. We have that in common.

"It's not really that simple," says Shawna, her thumb still in her mouth. "I think that everyone can change. Not everyone does, but some people do. And if people do change, don't they deserve another chance?"

"But shit happens to you when you are young and it shapes your brain. It impacts the way you look at things and the choices you make," Miranda murmurs.

"Shawna's not saying it doesn't impact you, but we make our own choices. No one forced me to do the shit I did to end up in here and no one forced you, either. I know what happened to me and it messed me up. I think about it every day of my life and I will for the rest of my life. But I am not going to use it as an excuse," Alexa cuts in, waving her pencil about like a baton.

"It affects your subconscious! It makes you more likely to do bad things and get in trouble because that's all you saw growing up. And when we are teenagers, our brains are not formed yet, so we do things that we would not do if we thirty."

"It still sounds like you are making excuses. Just cause our brains aren't formed yet, that doesn't mean we don't know right and wrong. I know if I shoot somebody, I did something wrong."

"Exactly! It's black and white. Killing people is wrong and you should go to jail forever."

"But people can change in prison. I saw my Uncle Ron change in prison. He became a Christian and he is still serving life for killing someone."

"Just cause he became a Christian doesn't mean anything. Being religious doesn't take back anything. It's like oh, so now you believe in God and you think you are forgiven, so you want to get out?"

"I'm not saying let them out, I am just saying their case should go up for review every few years," Alexa repeats calmly. "Doesn't everyone deserve a chance to try again?"

"So they can get out and kill more people? What if that was your family member?" Vanessa demands.

"Family or not, people deserve more changes. You can't just feel one way about a rule because your family is involved. You can't make it personal."

"If you do the crime, that's it. You should do the time. You are done. Unless you are crazy, you are responsible," Vanessa shouts, hitting the table for emphasis.

"That's the kind of mentality that got us in here in the first place," Alexa shakes her head. "And what about you? What if it was your family member? Would you honestly want your brother to do life in prison?"

"If he killed someone, that's the price he should pay. It would break my heart, but he has to pay the price."

"How does that even make sense though? You take someone else's life and then the state takes away yours? I get the whole eye for an eye thing, but it still won't bring the dead person back." Miranda's has been far away for days, floating on the periphery. Her mother has drifted into a medically induced coma, the cancer ravaging her body like a carnivorous monster. She was allowed to leave the hall yesterday to visit her mother in the ICU. They made her visit her mom in shackles, her wrists and ankles bound.

"I guess prison doesn't really make anything right or even better. It just makes the system think they taught someone a lesson." Alexa runs her hand through the chopped chunks of her hair. Her shaved head was starting to fill in with bursts of sandy blond hair. She would be leaving us soon to go to a home for foster youth in Sacramento. She wanted to grow her hair out, but for some reason it was coming in unevenly and gave her the appearance of a chrysanthemum that just woke up.

"We are all responsible for our actions," Vanessa flatlines. A hollow missive uttered by many and echoed by even more. "I took responsibility for my actions. That's why I am here."

"You didn't take responsibility for shit! You got caught! That's not the same thing," Shawna laughs. "If you had turned yourself in, that would be one thing. Don't play like you are some great, noble person."

If looks could kill Shawna would be dead right now. Vanessa snarls and flips her brown banner of hair over her left eye, the antithesis of a white flag.

"It's not a question of being responsible. It's understanding that we all come with experiences that affect how we act," Alexa whispers. Her eyes are looking out to a horizon only she can see. "My mom was a junkie. I was born addicted. When I was learning to walk, I stepped on one of my mom's needles. My foot got all infected but my mom didn't want to take me to the hospital because she was afraid she would get in trouble. When she finally did, I had a fever and I was close to death. They took me away from my mom. And I blamed everyone else for years: the hospital, the cops, child services."

"So because your mom was a junkie, you think that makes you being one okay?" Vanessa demands. "You gotta take responsibility for your own life, girl."

"My mom never took responsibility for what she did to my whole fucking life! I can accept the consequences for everything I did! No one forced a needle into this arm!" Alexa is out of herself, holding up her limpid right arm like a burden of proof. "But my mom never even said she was sorry. The last time I saw her was in a courtroom and she wouldn't even look at me! I don't know if it was out of guilt or anger, but do you know what it feels like when your own mom won't even look at you? I didn't even do anything wrong. I was just there. And even that was her fault."

"We are all someone's fault." Miranda's voice swells darkly, a murder of crows in a cold white classroom.

June 2

Kids will write their autobiographies, intentionally or otherwise. Their histories and selves, wounds and victories, shortcomings and wisdom bleed into their writing. It saturates the lines, soaking through like the poinsettia of a gunshot blast through white cotton.

We were doing expository essays this week, the kids allowed to choose any topic they felt they could explain to another. Zig-zagging through the aisles, a symphony of ideas blossoms up from the hard wood of their desks: how to end a relationship, how to make dinner for your family, how to rebuild a Mustang engine.

The title of Eduardo's paper is 'How to be a Failure'. I have to downshift as I get close to him, idle softly. Too often backfire has been gunfire for him. There is a foggy force field shrouding him, requiring slow and patient navigation in order to land safely on the surface of him. Sudden words are like sudden movements around a dog who has been kicked for years. Shaking his head ever so slightly, he doesn't raise it as I slide into a desk beside him. He doesn't want to come out to meet me. And that's okay. But I will sit at the door of the cage until he does.

"This is quite a topic, Eduardo." Hand out, palm down, no eye contact. "I like it. Very honest and personal. If I saw this in a stack, I would want to read this one first."

He squeezes his eyes together, wishing me away, yet his shoulder slides down an inch exposing a sliver of the neck that he keeps covered when people get close to him.

"The title is powerful. Makes me think that if I read it, I would learn something." I am on my knees here, begging him to believe that I will not smack his face as he turns it up towards me. Almost nine months with Eduardo and I am still standing at square one every time I need something from him. He needs proof of my safety every day. "Can you tell me what happens next?"

He lifts his head, eyelids rising like a funeral flag on its sad ascent to half-mast. It takes everything in him just to do this, breathing alone sucking him down to the bone.

"Can you write down a few things that you think make your life a failure? Can you take that first step? I will be right here and you can stop when you need to."

He rolls his pencil between his fingers, fitting his nail into the teeth marks he has left on the wood. He flips it from a joint into a fork, gathering breath as he begins to feed himself to the paper. *Join a gang. Become a drug addict. Hang out with criminals. Stop going to school. Turn off everything that makes you feel anything.* He sets the pencil down, cupping his small hand over it, like he doesn't trust what it is capable of.

"What makes you think that doing these things makes you a failure?" I have to lure him to the door of this, let him search my fingers for threats.

"Cause that's what I did." His voice rips open like a scab. "Look at me. I'm in a gang, I got kicked out of school, my mom is scared for her life when she isn't too high to know what the hell is going on, my dad hasn't called me in fifteen years, and I spend all my time in jail or rehab. If that's not being a failure, I don't know what is."

"What was the first bad step?" Like any snowflake could ever be blamed for an avalanche.

"Joining a gang. Nothing good has come from that. At least when I am high, I can draw. I can make the hurt into art with a pen. But it's kind of hard to hold a pen and a gun at the same time."

Across the room, Jose's arm goes up. Eduardo nods that he will be okay in this minefield for a few moments. I grasp his little hand for a second, telling him silently that I will be back. Eduardo needs me to stay far away and never leave his side, all at once.

Jorge slips into the empty desk beside Eduardo, stealthy as a rattler in high desert grass. "Listen, you junkie. I don't want to hear you talking shit on the family. Watch your mouth or it may not work so well one day."

Eduardo's gaze is three hundred miles away in a place that he can never get to but has been moving towards since birth. All Iago in the ear, Jorge continues to murmur until he sees me approaching.

"You giving Eduardo some advice, Jorge?" We are face to face on a battlefield, a wounded prisoner on the ground between us. We both want him, but for entirely different reasons.

"I was just asking him how to spell something." Jorge is all snake-oil smiles and used car salesman gleam.

"I'm sure. Now get back to your seat before I forget that I am a teacher for a minute." I return to Eduardo's side but it's too late. The drawbridge is closed. Try your luck with the alligators in the moat. "Eduardo, come back."

"These were my choices." He scrawls a large X over his words and flips his paper over.

"Yes, exactly. They were. Past tense. You can choose something else now. You're still alive. You can leave the drugs and the gang. It's not too late." This is a sad scramble up a wet rope, twine ripping into my hands as I try to reach a safe ground with him.

"I made a commitment," he murmurs. He is a lost explorer in snowdrifts up around his waist. It's so cold, and he just wants to sleep. Just to lay down for a moment in the silent white, just to rest.

"You made a commitment to violence and death. Is that what you want your life to be about?" This is a last second hanging from this branch, my arm shaking and fingers unlatching one by one.

"I made a promise. And I keep my promises even if they kill me."

June 9

As the teaching staff, we only get a small percentage of the information that the probation staff gets, even though we all deal with the same kids. And the kids usually know more than all the adults combined. They have their ears to the floor and the walls, communicating in ways that we cannot even begin to understand.

The newspaper carries bits of stories, as well. Usually if one of my students' names is in the news, it's not a positive thing. The article was small, no more than a paragraph, in the online version of the local paper: 'Teenager Shot to Death'. This kid was young enough to have been one of ours, his body found in a local city. No name was provided.

I didn't have to wait past first period to find out. The boys file in, somber and disheveled. Hair uncombed, eyes puffy from lack of sleep and crying, they had obviously found out about this last night. No one bothers to get pencils or journals. They are zombies, falling wordlessly into their places.

"Who was it?" I ask. My heart sticks in my throat like a piece of steak. I already know. Part of me already knows. Please let them tell me I am wrong.

"Antonio."

The room spins and my stomach seizes up. Please, not Antonio. Not the Antonio who cried over dead plants. Not the Antonio who was trying to pull away from the death machine of his gang. Not the Antonio who had every reason not to be hopeful and yet still was.

"Do you want to talk about it?"

They won't be producing any work today. Not that I can teach. Everything I have to offer is useless and empty.

"It's just bullshit, you know?" Juan croaks, tears filling his eyes.

"Don't talk about it," Jorge snarls.

"I need to talk about it. Fucking respect that, will you?" Juan's voice is thick with sadness but cracking.

"You don't need to talk to her. She doesn't get it. What do you care, Miss Wehr? You didn't know him like we did." Jorge is setting up crime scene tape around their experience. He does not want me past these parameters.

"You are right. I don't get it. I don't get why any of you would want to be part of something that killed people you love. And I did know Antonio. Not as well or for as long as you guys did, but I still loved him."

"Yea, but you people don't get it."

"You people? I am not people. I am just me."

"We grew up together, you know? We played together and we went to the same after-school programs together. He was a good guy," Jose says. "They won't put that in the news. All they will talk about is how he was in a gang and how he was gunned down in an alley like a fucking dog."

"I heard one of the staff talking about him this morning. Saying it was going to happen, that it was just a matter of time. It's like as soon as you are in a gang, you stop being human to everyone. Like because he is Mexican and in a gang, he deserves to die. And because he is poor and lives in the ghetto, no one really gives a shit," Juan murmurs, his tears falling freely to the desk. "They expect us to die and then they wonder why we do."

I wish I could argue with him, but it's true. Our societal empathy policy is discriminatory. If a teenager is shot and killed, there is usually some community outrage, some sort of outcry. But if the child was in a gang, there seems to be much more of a 'well, he asked for it' sort of attitude.

"They won't talk about how loyal he was or how funny he was or how much he loved his family. Just the gang shit," snarls Carlos, refusing to look away from the wall.

"He wasn't that loyal," Jorge mutters. His eyes are glassy and cold, having seen so much loss. This is just another thing that is gone. Then it hit me: Antonio had been taken out by his own gang. He was trying to leave and they would have rather him be dead and theirs than alive and free.

"So he deserves to die? He was trying to save his life and your fucking gang took it from him! Like if his life wasn't completely yours, it was worthless! And you have the nerve to talk about loyalty. Gangs know nothing about loyalty! You weren't loyal to Antonio the person, you were only loyal to Antonio the Norteno! Your gang saw him as a tool to be used and thrown away when he stopped being useful to you!" Tears are pouring down my face,

229

anything besides hysteria and heartbeat having escaped me. "Say something!"

"You don't understand how the streets work." Jorge's voice is something rising from the bowels of him, like the essence of possession. He lowers his eyes. He is a shut down building, doors locked and boarded up. I can't get to him anymore. Maybe I never did.

And this is the most sickening, the most profoundly wretched feeling. Sobbing and miserable, I see myself now as they and everyone else must. I am one person, one idealistic, hopeful idiot standing before a machine and trying to stop it by laying flowers in the cogs. There is a divide between us that I can't possibly traverse. I can love my students until it breaks me, but it won't save them. Love isn't enough.

*****

A few days later the same online local paper updated the article. They added two things to it: Antonio's full name and the fact that his death was believed to be gang related. As if the gang milieu somehow justified the death of an eighteen year old. I find the whole mention of a murdered person's gang entanglements a bit tactless. The police are the only ones who need to know that the victim was associated with a gang. Why put it in the newspaper for all of the victim's family and friends to read? It's dishonoring to the deceased.

All of us teachers had our memories of Antonio. We have all had our moments of success and frustration with him as he wove his way through the system. It saddened us to see such a bright boy so completely dedicated to self-destruction. We had hopes for his future, but all were tinged with a sour note of fear. We saw what was in his future. Maybe not to this extent, but if there was not a radical change, something was going to happen. And it did. We watched his death in slow motion for eight months. And there was nothing we could do. It was like watching a movie that you already know the ending to.

When Osama bin Laden was killed, Juan said, "I know he was a bad guy, but isn't it wrong to be happy that anyone gets killed?"

The example is an extreme one, but the comment stuck with

230

me. Why do we as a society get such an almost elated feeling when we feel that a 'bad guy' got what was coming to him? We seem to have confused revenge with justice.

I wish I could put this journey into one succinct sentence, tie everything up in a heartfelt, inspiring closing sentence. But being a teacher in Juvenile Hall is a Mobius strip. Everything bleeds into everything else. You get the same students in and out, over and over. It's always and never the same. Some of my colleagues have been teaching the same kids for eight years. Having someone in your life for a year is a hard enough attachment to break, but spending eight years with a student would make their final departure more heartbreaking than I could bear. I have already taught countless sets of siblings and cousins. Sometimes we have two or three members of the same family in at a time.

So much has happened this year. So many students have sat in these desks. And while I try to remember all of them, I cannot. There were some kids who were here so briefly, sat so quietly. I never even knew their names. And then they were gone.

I have learned more from my students, about life and hardship, strength and sorrow, joy and resilience, then I have in the twenty-seven years leading up to this. Anything I have learned, any way in which I have strengthened or grown or become a better teacher, I owe to my students.

It's a mixed feeling when a student never returns. Wearing my optimist hat, I can convince myself it is because they stopped getting in trouble. Maybe they are making better choices, doing better in school, staying away from drugs and gangs. Then the dark worry cloud comes back, reminding me that this may not be the case. They may be still miserable, still using, still on the streets, still being victimized or still victimizing others. They just haven't been caught yet.

Then there are the ones that have come back, some seven or eight times in the past year. As teachers, we chuckle and joke about how we are raising them and how much they must love jail because they keep coming back. But we are disappointed to see their names on the population sheet once again. And a little relieved, too. We know when they are with us, they are safe. No one is shooting at them, they aren't getting high or carrying guns, they aren't prostituting themselves or robbing people on the city bus. A lot of their parents have said that the only time they don't worry about their kids is when they are incarcerated because they at least know their babies are alive.

Release dates mean excitement for our students. They cross the days off on the calendar and remind us every day how many weeks they have left. Watching them walk out the door, a piece of my heart leaves with each one of them. Will I see them in my classroom again in a few weeks? Will I run into them somewhere on the outside and hear their stories of success and health and happiness? Will their name appear in a newspaper article, along with a funeral notice? Or, as is often the case, will they just disappear into the world, to fight and fall and hopefully rise and continue on? As a natural worrier, this may be the worst type of teaching job that I could have taken. I am terrified that people will not see their beauty or acknowledge their gifts or respect their weaknesses or honor them for how precious they are. May the world bless them and protect them as they grow and struggle and find their place.

THE END

Hannah Wehr has spent seven years teaching poetry, creative writing, and Language Arts in juvenile correctional facilities throughout California. She has spent six years as a performance poet, college lecturer, prison poetry panel member, and is the recipient of awards from the Los Angeles City Council for her assistance in the creation of The Hollywood Institute of Poetics. A contributing author to "What I Know Now: Writings From Inside" from Stanford University and author of "How To Start a Writing Program for Incarcerated Youth", Hannah lives in Northern California where she teaches English, Classic Film, and Drama at a juvenile detention facility in the Bay Area.

More About "Thugness Is A Virtue" –

'Hannah Wehr presents a bleak, scorchingly funny, to-the-bone account of her first year working in a juvenile detention center. Ostensibly about her teaching experiences, the book is also a stinging indictment of the entire juvenile prison system that repeatedly fails young inmates. Hannah makes compelling arguments for stripping down, re-defining and re-organizing the system. Read these young students' stories. Hear their voices. Be prepared for your heart to be broken and filled and broken and filled again. Hannah Wehr writes from the hip: an unsentimental, direct, clear and essential voice.'

~ **Sandra Hunter**, author of *Losing Touch*

'Hannah Wehr is going to break your heart. Her inside look at forgotten youth will pull you in a riptide of tight prose and never let go. Welcome to a rising star in the literary world who is fearless in how she bears witness.'

~ **Derrick Brown**, author of *Our Poison Horse*, Winner of the Texas Book of the Year Prize

'Hannah Wehr's *Thugness is a Virtue,* A Teacher's First Year in Juvenile Hall is a richly intense account of a dedicated teacher coming to grips with the reality of incarcerated youth. It gives the reader an honest view of the lives of many children and adults that go beyond surviving the rigorous obstacles of their environment. She brings voices to life in a manner that is respectful and validates those that take the time to share their story. Amazingly these children show a strong sense of hope and caring that touches the heart of those around them. Their resilience is remarkable and encouraging. It should motivate us to listen more and honor the many stories children carry with them everyday, and Wehr brings these stories to life in a vivid, lucid prose that is neither sentimental nor condescending.'

~ **Richard Modiano**, author of *Driving All The Horses at Once*, Executive Director at Beyond Baroque Literary Arts Center

A HISTORY OF BROKEN LOVE THINGS (2014)
by SB Stokes

YEAH, WELL... (2014) by Joel Landmine

DREAMS GONE MAD WITH HOPE (2014) by S.A. Griffin

CODE BLUE: A LOVE STORY (2014) by Jack Grisham

HOW TO TAKE A BULLET AND OTHER SURVIVAL
POEMS (2014) by Hollie Hardy

DEAD LIONS (2014) by A.D. Winans

SCARS (2014) by Nadia Bruce-Rawlings

STEALING THE MIDNIGHT FROM A HANDFUL OF DAYS
(2014) by Michele McDannold

WHEN I WAS A DYNAMITER, Or, How a Nice Catholic Boy
Became a Merry Prankster, a Pornographer, and a Bridegroom Seven
Times (2104) by Lee Quarnstrom

FORTHCOMING BOOKS ON PUNK HOSTAGE PRESS

WHERE THE ROAD LEADS (2015) by Diana Rose

SHOOTING FOR THE STARS IN KEVLAR (2015)
by Iris Berry

LONGWINDED TALES OF A LOW PLAINS DRIFTER (2015)
by A. Razor

EVERYTHING IS RADIANT BETWEEN THE HATES (2015)
by Rich Ferguson

GOOD GIRLS GO TO HEAVEN, BAD GIRLS GO
EVERYWHERE (2015) by Pleasant Gehman

BOULEVARD OF SPOKEN DREAMS (2015) by Iris Berry

DANGEROUS INTERSECTIONS (2015) by Annette Cruz

DRIVING ALL OF THE HORSES AT ONCE (2015)
by Richard Modiano

DISGRACELAND (2015)
by Iris Berry & Pleasant Gehman

AND THEN THE ACID KICKED IN (2015)
by Carlye Archibeque

BODIES: BRILLIANT SHAPES (2015) by Kate Menzies

BORROWING SUGAR (2015) by Susan Hayden

BASTARD SONS OF ALPHABET CITY (2015) by Jon Hess

THE REDHOOK GIRAFFE & OTHER BROOKLYN
TALES (2015) by James A. Tropeano III

PURO PURISMO (2015) by A. Razor

IN THE SHADOW OF THE HOLLYWOOD SIGN (2015)
by Iris Berry

SIRENS (2015) by Larry Jaffe

Made in the USA
Lexington, KY
13 December 2014